P9-CCC-385

READY, SET-UP, COOK

A SIMPLE GUIDE TO SETTING UP,
AND CREATING, YOUR COOKING
ENVIRONMENT

Alison Porter

authorHOUSE®

AuthorHouse™
1663 Liberty Drive, Suite 200
Bloomington, IN 47403
www.authorhouse.com
Phone: 1-800-839-8640

© *2008 Alison Porter. All rights reserved.*

No part of this book may be reproduced, stored in a retrieval system, or transmitted by any means without the written permission of the author.

First published by AuthorHouse   7/14/2008

ISBN: 978-1-4343-9199-5 (sc)

Printed in the United States of America
Bloomington, Indiana

This book is printed on acid-free paper.

Dedication

This book is lovingly dedicated to my two wonderful children. Brad, who has always been my best and worst culinary critic. Kailey, who has encouraged and pushed me during this endeavor. I love you both

And to Ben, who was a wonderful friend, I will miss you always.

Acknowledgements

There are several individuals and groups I must gratefully acknowledge.

I would like to thank the Sorority core board for the opportunity to cook in the most wonderful kitchen I can imagine, and for their constant love and support.

A thanks and hug to the beautiful young ladies I have had the lucky opportunity to know and cook for. Their suggestions were of great value to the format of this book. I love each and every one of you that I have had the pleasure of cooking for.

I would like to acknowledge Yvonne who recognized my potential. I would like to thank Maggie who continued the support of, and belief in me.

Thanks and love to my dear friends and family of SoWal.

Thank you to my uncle Steve who first planted the seed for this book in my mind. Thanks mom and dad for the sanctuary of your home to help me get this project started.

Lastly a big thanks to a friend who has been a sounding board, a supporter and a shoulder for many years, Peter Cherico.

Introduction

I guess the best way to begin this book is to explain it. My uncle first gave me the suggestion to create this book about a year and a half ago. I agreed it was a great idea, but it took me this long to bring it to reality. For the past four years, I have had the joy of being a chef for a sorority. I have learned quite a lot and it is my hope to share some of these discoveries. This book is meant to be a guide for setting up your own kitchen and to be comfortable in that kitchen. I hope that this book will be beneficial to anyone that is setting up a first time kitchen, or those that need some new suggestions.

Whenever I have prepared myself to write anything of importance I have ended up having a conversation in my head. I mull over my words for days, sometimes even weeks. In my preparation for this book; I have had the same conversations in my mind. These conversations were with you, reader. This is how I have decided to write this book, as if I am actually having a conversation with you. It is not fancy nor always grammatically correct. I write this book just as I would talk to you. My intent is to make what I say understandable, easy and friendly.

The first thing I want you to understand is that setting up a kitchen, cooking and entertaining are not a scary thing. I hope that you will come to realize this while using this book and you will become comfortable with the kitchen. You don't have to spend a lot of money to achieve a well functioning kitchen.

The recipes included in this book are ones that the sorority girls have asked for, or are ones that are tried and true. Most of them are my own, or are recipes which I have modified to meet my needs. Any of the recipes can be made fat free or organic, simply by substituting fat free ingredients or organic ingredients. I will say that I would rather use a small amount of the real thing (eg. butter vs margarine, real mayonnaise vs fat free). The choice to use fat free, low fat or the "real" thing is totally up to you.

When mentioning name brands, stores or products, I am not discounting other counterparts, they are simply the ones that I know about and use. Also, I would like to say that these are my suggestions based on the knowledge that I have gained throughout the years. Not every point in this book is going to fit you, but hopefully will jog your own culinary creativity.

Have fun with your kitchen; enjoy creating your cooking space. The kitchen has always been the life blood of the home. Memories and traditions are created within the framework of the kitchen. The old saying "familiarity breeds contempt" is not true in this case. With the kitchen "familiarity breeds contentment"! I hope you enjoy this book.

Table of Contents

KITCHEN SET UP

My intention with this section of the book is to familiarize you with the needs of your kitchen. Setting up your kitchen does not have to be expensive. The initial investment can be costly, but you don't have to do it all at once. You don't have to spend a ton of money when purchasing utensils, appliances or kitchen wear. All of my suggestions are just that, suggestions. I have found that you don't have to buy the most expensive things. Expensive is not always better. I believe that you should explore your options. Dollar stores, discount stores, drug stores and even thrift stores are inexpensive alternatives. When purchasing food goods, use coupons, shop sales and buy store brands.

Again I want to reiterate that the stores or products that I mention are the ones that I am familiar with or are in my area. Every where there are many wonderful stores and brands, find the ones that suit your needs.

Utensils

My belief on utensils is not to necessarily purchase the most expensive. You never know which ones you will truly need or use. This is a guide to what you will need at one time or another. If you use an item once or twice a month, and you purchase that item for a dollar, it might not last forever, but you will not have spent much on it. You can simply buy another for a dollar. If it turns out to be an item you use frequently, then you can purchase a more expensive one at a later date.

The following list is a general guide. I have included some pricing that I have observed while conducting my research. These are not in any particular order, just whatever popped into my mind at the time, perhaps by importance in my own kitchen.

I like to find fun containers for my counter top to keep utensils in. You can find these containers in many different places; thrift stores, antique shops, specialty shops and craft stores.

Rubber Spatula: These are a must have! There are two types, and I suggest you have each.

- **Flat spatulas:** These are great for scraping bowls and pans. Ideal when transferring batters, dips, spreads dressings and marinades. The spatula gets every little drop.

In a local dollar store, where everything is actually a dollar you can purchase a set of three spatulas for, yep, a dollar. Other dollar stores have the same product for around two or three dollars.

- **Spoonulas:** Rubber spatulas in the shape of a spoon. They are good for the same uses as the flat spatula, but with added bonuses. You can easily stir sticky things such as rice without them sticking. I have a very hard time using metal spoons to do the same job. The rubber cuts through the sticky food without getting "clogged". The spoonula is also great for folding ingredients into each other. This is where I would splurge. Buy a good quality. I suggest one that is 3-4 inches in length and 3-3 ½ inches in width. I also recommend purchasing a spoonula that is heat proof. These are ideal for sautéing and stirring, especially in nonstick pans.

Spatulas: Used for flipping food. Purchase ones for non-stick cook wear and a small metal one for general use. Also purchase one which can be used on non-stick pans.

Wire Wisk: Another favorite utensil. It is invaluable when making sauces, dressings, dips and gravies. I have several different sizes; an 11 inch long x 3 inch round, a 10 inch long x 2 inch round and a 7 ½ inch long x 2 inch round. You won't need all these, just the last two are necessary. I have included the whisk in the glossary. It will help explain what a whisk is and the best way to use it. Here again, whisks can be purchased in discount stores for a dollar or more.

Wooden Spoon: Good for stirring food when using non-stick cook wear. If you don't have a heat resistant rubber spoon, a wooden spoon will do fine, it just won't scrape out the food very well. I found a set of 4 wooden spoons at the Dollar Tree (everything is a dollar). Most other dollar stores and discount stores have them for close to the same price.

Tongs: I used to call these "clickey-clackies". Tongs are an essential utensil, it's like having an extra pair of hands. Tongs are good for turning meat and tossing salads. I use tongs when serving green beans or any long vegetable that is too big for a serving spoon. I also serve spaghetti noodles with tongs. There are many more uses. Tongs come in many different sizes. You can also purchase tongs with heat resistant tips for use on non-stick pans. If you find tongs for a dollar, buy 2 or 3 of different sizes. You can't have too many tongs.

Soup Ladle: For serving soup, stews, gravies or chilies.

Serving Spoons: Purchase a set that includes spoons that are solid and ones with holes. Two of each is a good amount.

Knives: I recommend a discount store or a bedding and bath store when purchasing knives. The knives I recommend are a paring knife, a small chef knife, a serrated bread knife and a 7 inch santoku knife. A paring knife is a good all purpose knife. A chef's knife is used for chopping. I do not recommend a serrated chef's knife. The chef's knife is good for chopping because it is a bit curved and allows for the rocking motion needed to chop. A serrated bread knife is useful when slicing bread and is ideal for slicing tomatoes. If you can find an offset bread knife buy it.

Colander: Good for draining large amounts of food such as pasta and potatoes. I also like the wire mesh colanders which come in several different sizes. Use to drain canned beans and peas, rinsing fruits and vegetables.

Wire Mesh Strainer: You can always use a hand held wire mesh strainer. Strain sauces, canned goods, small amounts of pasta, you name it. I also use it to sift flour with other dry ingredients.

Potato Peeler: Used for peeling potatoes, cucumbers and apples.

Can Opener: I detest electric can openers. I have always used a good can opener. Do not scrimp on this item. I use a "swing-a-way". There are also can openers available that take the top off of a can without the sharp edge.

Cutting Board: A good cutting board is an essential item in your kitchen. I always purchase poly boards. I do not like glass or the plastic roll-up cutting boards. I can think of nothing more annoying than cutting and chopping against glass. Wood is a good choice as well, but tends to be more expensive. You also must be careful with wood, it is porus. You have to keep a wood cutting board sanitized or use one for meats and another for fruits and vegetables. When buying cutting boards, I recommend you purchase two sizes, an 8 x 10 for small cutting jobs, and an 11 x 14 for larger jobs. Always place a damp paper towel, dish cloth or grip liner underneath the cutting board before using. I will address the proper use and care of cutting boards in the safety and sanitization section.

Measuring Spoons: Dollar and discount stores.

Measuring Cups: Dollar and discount stores.

Four Cup Measurer: Dollar and discount stores.

Egg Slicer: An item that you really might not use too often, but it is worth it to buy a good one. Ideal for slicing eggs, and chopping them too. Slice the egg length wise and then flip it to slice it width wise, use in potato salad, egg salad or chef's salad. If you have firm strawberries an egg slicer is ideal for slicing strawberries. I have not tested this, but I am sure it would work well on kiwis too.

Funnel: Used to transfer liquids into small mouthed containers.

Round Cookie Cutter: Because you never know what uses you will find. I have used it for my mini puff pastry pockets, cutting bread rounds and cutting out pie dough rounds. I recommend several different sizes.

Scissors: Kitchen or regular scissors. I have both, but at work I have always used just plain ol' scissors. I use scissors to cut just about anything and everything.

Pizza Cutter: Beside the obvious, these are great for cutting pita rounds, quesadillas and flat bread into triangles. If you purchase one, make sure it is a larger one.

Microplane: Used for grating cheese, ginger, onion and zesting citrus.

Pastry Brush: The new trend in pastry brushes are rubber bristles. I was skeptical at first, but my aunt gave me one that she purchased at a dollar store. It works great and it is so much more sanitary. The brush cleans up easily in the dishwasher. You can also use a regular brush which looks like a small paint brush. Used for brushing breads and meats with oils, marinades and sauces. Do not use this brush for the grill. There are long handled brushes for this purpose.

Zyliss Cheese Grater: A hand operated grater. My sister-in-law would not be happy with me if I did not include this item. It is an essential part of an Italian kitchen. It is wonderful for grating hard cheese such as Parmesan and Romano.

Rolling Pin: At some point you will need one of these. I have the regular wooden rolling pin, but they also come in metal and marble. Follow instructions when using rolling pins. Marble is the best pin since it is a good material for rolling out dough. The marble stays cool and dough does not stick to it as much as it does with wood. Usually you have to use a lot of flour when using a wooden rolling pin to avoid sticking.

Pot Holders: Buy a good quality pot holder, one that works. Square pot holders or mitts are good, just be sure they are heat resistant.

Trivet: A ceramic or metal disk used for placing hot pots and pans on. A trivet lets you rest your meat and casserole dishes and not burn the counter top. I recommend a trivet that is grated and a little bit raised, it will allow for air flow beneath the pot or pan for even cooling.

Hands: One of the most wonderful and useful kitchen utensils you can have are your hands. I always use gloves when using my hands to mix salads (tuna and potato salad, etc.), tossing green salads.

Appliances

When it comes to appliances, I am referring to small appliances. I visited a local drug store chain and found many of the small appliances that I list here for sale at about ten dollars a piece.

Food Chopper: I recommend a small chopper or food processor. Invaluable for chopping, blending and mincing small amounts of food. I use mine for chopping peeled garlic, mincing onion and bell pepper and finely chopping nuts. A ten dollar item at the drug store.

Hand Mixer: Use for mixing many different dishes. Cakes, puddings, mashed potatoes, whipped cream, whipped egg whites, spreads and dips. A ten dollar item.

Four Cup Coffee Maker: Ten dollar item. Ideal for one cup. It says 4 cup, but believe me, it only makes one. I usually only drink one cup anyway. If you need a larger coffee maker, there are 8 cup capacity makers available for around fifteen dollars.

Crock Pot: Depending on your use, you can buy a very small one with a 2 quart capacity, or a larger one with a 4-5 quart capacity. I don't use mine very often, but it is nice to have on hand. The small crockpot is available for 10 dollars. If you buy a larger one, make sure it has a removable insert and a plastic, heat resistant top.

Toaster Oven: I prefer one of these to a traditional toaster. I use mine constantly. I make almost anything in it that I would in the oven, unless it is something that has to bake for longer than 10 minutes. I use my toaster oven as a broiler, toaster and to reheat leftovers such as pizza. My toaster oven was about 20 dollars.

Microwave: If your home or apartment does not include a built in microwave a small one is a necessity. Buy the smallest and least expensive one you can find. I never use my microwave to cook with, but it is great for heating, melting and defrosting.

Blender: I love my blender. If you splurge with any small appliance, do it on a good blender. I puree soups, sauces, vinaigrettes and smoothies in my blender. Lets not forget about frozen drinks. I recommend a blender that is glass.

Deep Fat Fryer: I have a fryer that has a temperature gauge on it. Most foods are fried at 350 degrees. I do not use this appliance very often, but I love to make fried chicken and fish from time to time. Fryers are not mandatory by any means, but I had to mention it, because it is a fun thing to have when you need it. I would consider it a splurge. I do not recommend using the frying method often, but for the best french fries and fried chicken, you can't beat a fryer.

Bakeware

I must confess, my collection of bakeware is a hodgepodge of items. I have accumulated various bakeware over the years, but I usually end up using the same items over and over. If storage is limited, choose a few things from my list that you know you will need right away, and add as needed.

Baking Pan: At one time I used cookie sheets which are flat baking pans. I now prefer to use a baking pan also called a jelly roll pan or sheet pan. The sheet pan has a shallow lip.

The sheet pan fulfills the majority of my baking needs. I have two sizes in my kitchen; a 9x13 and a 12x17. The smaller one is a non-stick surface and used for small baking like toasting nuts. The large one is the one I use most often. I purchased it at Sam's Club. The half sheet pans (as they are called) are restaurant grade and come in sets of two. If you have access to a Sam's or Costco store, you can buy sheet pans in a set of two. Find a friend to share the cost. The sheet pans can also be found at bedding and bath stores.

Casserole Pan: A glass dish used for baking casseroles, lasagna, etc. Casserole pans do not have covers. At the discount store, I found a set of three sizes for 5 dollars. The set consisted of a 9x13 inch, an 8x11 inch and a 6x9 inch pan.

Covered Baking Dish: A glass baking dish with a cover used for baking foods that require a cover. Baking dishes are usually deep and good for baking rice dishes, stews and casseroles which need a lid. Baking dishes are usually round. I recommend two sizes, a 7 inch round and a 9 inch round. Baking dishes can be found at discount stores and some dollar stores. Probably the most popular are the Pyrex brand or Anchor.

Dutch Oven: A large pot which is usually made of cast iron and can be used on the stove top or in the oven. Dutch ovens have tight fitting lids. I use a dutch oven to begin the cooking process on the stove top and finish cooking in the oven. Some of the dishes I use the dutch oven for are paella, jambalaya and beef stew. A dutch oven is not a necessary item to have, but at some future date it is a good thing to have in your bakeware collection.

Muffin Pan: I think everyone should have a muffin pan. You can use muffin pans for much more than just making muffins. An inexpensive substitute are aluminum muffin pans found at grocery and discount stores. Aluminum muffin tins require paper muffin cups. If you buy a metal muffin tin, purchase non-stick. I also highly recommend purchasing mini muffin tins. I use my minis for blue cheese biscuits bites.

Cake and Pie Pans: I recommend two standard cake pans and one pie pan, non-stick.

Bread Pan: A small, deep rectangular pan used for baking breads. I don't use this very often, but it is good to have. Can also be used for meat loaf and baking corn bread.

Roasting Pan: A shallow metal pan used to roast meats. Purchase a pan with a metal rack. The purpose of the rack is to keep meat off the bottom of the pan, allowing air flow and even cooking. The rack can also be used to rest baked dishes on to keep the bottom of the dish from getting soggy. Pies, casseroles, cakes, etc.

Mixing Bowls: Good for many uses. I have a set of 3 glass mixing bowls. The three sizes are 7 inch, 8 ½ inch and 10 inch round. I also have several metal mixing bowls. I recommend a larger bowl for mixing salads and larger quantity foods. You can usually find a larger bowl at a dollar store made of plastic.

Baking Stone: Baking stones are a wonderful item. Stones come in several shapes and sizes. I recommend a pizza stone. The stone is excellent for putting a nice crisp crust on pizza and for keeping the pizza hot for a long period of time. A stone can not be put in the dishwasher nor can you wash it. Stones are porus and will absorb the soap. Rinsing and scraping a stone is the way to clean it. Stones become "seasoned" with use. Stones can be found at specialty stores and bedding and bath stores.

Aluminum Pans: Whenever I have to take a baked dish to a function, I always use an aluminum pan. Aluminum pans are ideal because you don't have to worry about having to take the pan home. Aluminum pans come in many different shapes and sizes and can be found at most dollar and grocery stores. A word of caution aluminum pans are not very sturdy, so place the pan on top of a baking sheet before baking. Transport hot pans on the same baking sheet.

Silpat Mat: A nonstick baking and counter top mat, which does not need greasing of flouring. You can use a silpat for baking cookies, etc. in the oven or rolling dough on the counter top. Silpat mats can be found at bedding and bath stores.

Cookware

Cookware purchasing is a bit of a challenge. There are so many products out there today. I am of the opinion that expensive is not always the best. Years ago I received a set of expensive cookware which some friends insisted was the best. They loved how easily it cleaned up. I, however, did not care about clean up, I cared how well it cooked. This was very expensive cookware and it did not cook well at all. Perhaps it would have been better if it had been the nonstick set, but even then it would not justify the price.

With my cookware, just as with my bakeware, I have a hodgepodge of items. What I will recommend here are several different options. I visited a discount store and got some prices on sets and individual items. My suggestions are just that, suggestions to you so that you can choose what best fits your needs. If you are not sure, then I suggest buying a few necessary items and then add as needed. Another option is buy an inexpensive set and add individual items as needed. Another thing to consider is how the cookware is made. I prefer nonstick for pans and metal interior for pots. Unfortunately, sets come in one or the other.

My recommendation is to buy a nonstick set and purchase a few metal interior pots. Make sure the handles are coated with some sort of heat resistant material. Wood is nice, but can burn and eventually the handles will begin to loosen and wobble. Metal handles can become hot and burn your hand.

Sauté Pan: This pan comes in various sizes and has curved edges. I almost always use sauté pans as opposed to frying pans. I prefer a nonstick sauté pan which is ideal for browning meats and vegetables. I make a lot of stir fry dishes and a sauté pan is the best for this Individual sauté pans run around 5-7 dollars depending on size. A set of three sauté pans runs about 21 dollars at the discount store (nonstick). This set is an 8 inch, 10 inch and 12 inch.

Fry Pan: This pan has straight sides and is good for cooking a simmering foods and of course frying meats and vegetables. If it has an oven safe handle and finish you can braise meats on the stove top and finish them off in the oven. (Works well with chicken and fish). At the discount store I found a 4 quart (10 ½ inch) fry pan for 20 dollars.

Sauce Pot: Sauce pots come in many different sizes ranging from a 1 quart capacity all the way up to 8 quart capacity. Sauce pans normally come with a lid. Your kitchen should have at least 2 or 3 sizes of sauce pans.

Grill Pan: This is a flat pan with ridges on it. I had never used one of these, but when I moved 2 years ago, I no longer had a gas grill. I missed the grill. My dad was using a grill pan to cook steak on one of my visits to my parents. The steak, while not as good as a true grilled steak, was very good. I purchased a grill pan for myself and use it frequently for steaks, burgers, fish, chicken and shrimp. Grill pans run about 20 dollars at a bedding and bath store. This is not a mandatory item, but a good one to have.

Griddle: This is a flat, low rimmed pan with a handle. It is ideal for cooking pancakes, french toast and grilled cheese sandwiches. It is usually square and can fit 4 pieces of bread at a time. I also have a long grill pan that does not have a handle. This pan can accommodate 6 pieces of bread, however you have to place it vertically, covering two burners on your stove top. A griddle is not mandatory, but something for the future.

Stock Pot: This is a large pot that can be used for making large amounts of food. They are usually 10 quart capacity or more. Most include a lid. These tend to be expensive so save this purchase for when you find you really need it. Do not buy an aluminum pot. Stock pots should be made of a heavy, heat conducting material.

Cookware Sets: I Researched several different cookware sets at a discount store. I am still of the opinion that the cost of a cookware product is not so important. Most cookware will do the job, and if it is inexpensive and it needs replacing, then all you have to do is spend a little money to replace it. If you spend a fortune on "high quality" cookware, then you are pretty much stuck with it if you end up not liking it. I would save the expensive purchases for when you have found the right cookware set for you. At the discount store I found sets ranging from 23 dollars, for a 7 piece set, to 89 dollars, for a 12 piece set. A 35 dollar set was Tramontina which came with a red or black enamel outer finish and had a nonstick interior. This set contained an 8 inch sauté pan, 10 inch fry pan, 1 quart sauce pot, 2 quart sauce pot and a 5 quart dutch oven. The Wearever set was a 60 dollar 12 piece set. It had heat resistant material on the handles and lid pulls. All the sets were pretty much the same, the difference being the materials. A heavier pot and pan does perform better, but for most purposes, a less expensive set is acceptable as far as I am concerned.

Dinnerware, Flatware and Glassware

When it comes to these items, you can go basic, fun, eclectic or expensive. I recommend a place setting for eight when purchasing dinnerware and flatware.

Dinnerware: You can find dinnerware in all discount stores, department stores, bedding and bath stores, specialty stores and thrift stores. I recommend you do some shopping around and decide what is in your budget. If you go basic and inexpensive, 15 dollars for a 4 place setting set, then I would try to find a set that you like and matches your decor. If you go more expensive then my suggestion is to go with a neutral, something that you can use for years to come with any decor you have. If you really want to have some fun you can go to a thrift store and buy a varied combination of plates, bowls and mugs. You can also have some fun mixing and matching dinnerware at such stores as Pier One and Pottery Barn (this, however, can get expensive).

Flatware: Most sets have 5 pieces; a knife, a tea spoon, soup spoon, salad fork and food fork. They come with enough flatware for four people. Here again, you can spend as little as 10 dollars for a set of four, all the way up to 40 or 50 dollars. I would go with the 10 dollar sets at a discount store. I feel it is not an item that you need to spend a lot of money on initially. You want the flatware to be substantial, but it does not have to be expensive. Shop around and choose what fits within your budget.

Glassware: Most glass sets have 6 small glasses and 6 larger glasses. You will need glasses, but you should choose which ones suit your needs. Don't over do the glasses, they take up a lot of space and you really don't need that many. You can find sets for 10 dollars all the way up to 50 dollars. You can buy individual glasses at most stores. Wine glasses are something you will need to consider as well. Discount stores carry sets of 12 wine glasses for about 10 dollars.

Pantry

Setting up a pantry can be a fun endeavor. You will stock your pantry with the basics, which everyone needs, and you can add to your pantry to tailor it to your likes and dislikes. I will list staples that every pantry should include. Some of the ingredients might not be what you like, but they are nice to have on hand.

Oils: Olive oil and vegetable oil. I use extra virgin olive oil. Purchase a small bottle of olive oil. I use olive oil for most of my cooking, marinades and dressings. For vegetable oil, I use canola oil. These oils will usually stay good for many months . Sesame seed oil, used for asian dishes. I keep sesame seed oil in the refrigerator after opening. I also use a non-stick cooking spray. Keeping a small container of solid vegetable oil is good for baking needs.

Vinegars: I use several different vinegars. Most vinegars are inexpensive so I have a large variety.

- **Apple Cider Vinegar** I use this for many dressings and dishes.

- **White Vinegar** I use this when I make Asian dishes and for white sauce.

- **Rice Wine Vinegar** A mild vinegar used in Chinese cooking.

- **Red Wine Vinegar** I use this vinegar in dressings.

- **Balsamic Vinegar** This is my favorite vinegar of all time. I use it for almost everything. Many of my recipes in this book calls for balsamic vinegar. It is wonderful drizzled over a salad.

Pastas: Bow Tie, Angel Hair, Spaghetti and Penne.

Rice: Jasmine, long grain, a small bag of long grain and wild rice and yellow. I also keep a box of boil-in-bag rice in my pantry for quick rice.

Flour: All purpose unbleached. After opening I keep the bag in a gallon storage bag. I also keep a few boxes of Jiffy corn muffin mix.

Corn Starch: I use this for thickening a sauce without adding any flavoring. It has many other uses as well.

Sugar: I keep several types of sugar in my pantry. Brown sugar, powdered sugar and granulated sugar. I purchase the smallest amount. The granulated sugar I have is a one pound canister. I also use Splenda sugar packets for coffee and tea.

Peanut butter: I love peanut butter. At the sorority house we go through a jar a day. The girls use it for a dip for their apples and bananas. They also love it on graham crackers with grape jelly. I love to spread it on toast for a quick snack.

Snacks: I don't keep a lot of convenience snacks, but I do keep cashews and peanuts on hand. They are great for snacking. I like to pair nuts with craisins and raisins. I also like rice cakes and popcorn in the single size bags. You can decide what snacks you want to keep on hand. I do recommend you keep a box of your favorite crackers in the pantry.

Salsa: Chose your favorite brand. Refrigerate after opening.

Sweet pickle relish: I use sweet relish for tuna and egg salad. I also use it when I make tartar sauce. Refrigerate after opening.

Olives: Stuffed green olives, ripe olives whole and sliced, capers.

Roasted red peppers or pimentos: You will find many uses for this product, salad and pizza toppings, use with appetizers and main dishes.

Diced green chilies: A 4 ounce can. I use these for many different dishes.

Raisins and Craisins: (dried cranberries) I use these to snack on, put in rice and salads.

Jelly: Grape jelly, red currant jelly and blackberry jelly.

Baking Goods: Baking soda and baking powder.

Syrups: Pancake syrup, honey and corn syrup.

Canned Goods: Solid white tuna fish, chicken breast, petite diced tomatoes (14 oz), tomato paste (6 oz), tomato sauce (14 oz), grated Parmesan cheese (3 oz), golden bread crumbs (8 oz canister), Italian style bread crumbs (8 oz canister), pizza sauce.

Vegetables: I don't keep a lot of canned vegetables, but I do have black beans, refried beans, Lesueur peas and sliced mushrooms.

Soups: Cream of mushroom, tomato, beef broth, chicken broth. I also have Knorr bouillon cubes in beef and chicken. I normally have a box of Lipton onion soup mix and vegetable soup mix.

Liquid Flavoring: Worcestershire sauce, A-1 steak sauce, barbeque sauce, soy sauce, teriyaki sauce, tabasco, fish sauce. On the sweet side, pure vanilla extract.

Dry Seasoning: Taco seasoning mix, fajita seasoning mix, ranch dressing mix, good seasons dressing mix.

Herbs and Spices: I use a lot of herbs and spices. I have a large inventory. Some of these ingredients can be expensive, but they last a long time. Herbs are the leaves of a plant and spices are from the root, bark, seeds, stems and berry of a plant. Later on in this book I'll pair some spices and herbs with foods that they go well with. Some herbs and spices can be found in drug stores at a lower price than grocery stores. In my grocery store there is a separate section for herbs and spices from a supplier named Badia which are less expensive than the national brands. Badia does not carry all herbs and spices, but check them out before moving to the spice isle.

I have included some food and spice pairings in the cooking tip section of the book.

Spices:
- Ground mustard
- Cumin powder
- Chili powder
- Curry powder
- Garlic powder (I do not use garlic salt)
- Onion powder
- Paprika
- Red pepper flakes
- Cayenne Pepper
- Black pepper grinder
- Celery seed
- Sesame seed
- Ground ginger
- Ground cinnamon
- Ground nutmeg
- Whole cloves

Herbs:
- Parsley flakes
- Basil
- Thyme
- Oregano
- Rosemary (I do not use whole rosemary because it is too hard, but opt for ground or crushed)
- Dill weed

Refrigerator

How you stock your refrigerator will be more personal and tailored to your own needs, likes and dislikes. All I can do is make suggestions that you can follow for a well stocked refrigerator. You can add the things that you prefer and take away the things you don't like.

Half and Half: If you have a recipe that calls for milk, you can use half and half mixed with water to substitute. Half and half has a longer life than milk. I use half and half for my coffee.

Skim Milk or 2%: I don't use milk enough to keep some in my refrigerator, but if your lifestyle includes milk, keep a container in your refrigerator.

Sour Cream: I use reduced fat.

Cheese: I recommend a bag of shredded sharp Cheddar, Mozzarella and Parmesan. A package of Monterey Jack and Kraft cheese slices. I love Swiss cheese, so I sometimes buy sliced Swiss. I also like to keep a container of crumbled blue cheese. Cheese is a great thing to have on hand to snack on.

Eggs: I usually buy a six pack of eggs. I prefer organic, which are more expensive. I don't use eggs often, so the higher price is ok.

Butter: I buy two sticks of unsalted butter, refrigerate one and freeze the other. If you prefer margarine, it will stay in the refrigerator for a long time.

Bacon Grease: I don't use this often, but it is nice to have a small amount in your refrigerator or freezer. Store in a small freezer proof plastic container. I do like to use bacon grease for seasoning in some of my dishes.

Breads: I store my bread in the refrigerator to keep it fresh. I usually have small whole wheat pita bread, whole wheat flour tortillas and English muffins in my refrigerator. I also recommend keeping pizza crusts on hand. I purchase the small pizza crusts in a package of three. The two brands I have used are Boboli and Miss Mary's. You can also keep the crusts in the freezer. The larger shells are good when you want to make a large pizza.

Garlic: I buy the whole peeled garlic from the grocery. This garlic can be found in the produce section and is in a clear canister. I think it is a great product. I never use the already minced garlic in the jar. I will chop about ¼ cup of garlic cloves in my food chopper and store it in a small plastic storage container for about 5 days.

Vegetables: Buy the vegetables you like. I keep broccoli florets, cucumbers, green onions and celery for salads and snacking. I also like to keep a head of romaine. Celery can be stored in a water filled cup, which will keep it crisp. I use vegetables for salad, snacking, sandwiches and stir fry.

Fruits: Buy the fruits you like. I like Granny Smith apples, oranges, grapefruit, lemons, limes, grapes and strawberries.

Pickles: I always have a huge jar of Kosher Dill pickles in my refrigerator! I also keep pickle relish stored in the refrigerator after the jar has been opened.

Condiments: I keep mayonnaise, ketchup, mustard (yellow and spicy brown), salad dressings (Creamy Caesar and Light Ranch are what I keep), prepared horseradish and barbeque sauce.

Juices: I love V-8. It is also good to keep orange juice on hand.

Herbs: Herbs don't last long, so buy them as you need them. If you have some left over, the best way to store them is wrap them in damp paper towels and keep inside a ziplock bag. Parsley can be stored in a cup filled with water, place the parsley in the cup stem first, covered with plastic wrap.

Freezer

Just like your refrigerator, your freezer is going to be personalized by you. The following items are good to have in your freezer, but you can add to, or subtract from, this list.

Vegetables: I keep a big bag of chopped spinach for varied uses, a bag of corn and a bag of mixed vegetables (corn, carrots, beans and peas). After I have opened the bag, and if I have not used all of the contents, I store it in the freezer inside a freezer bag.

Nuts: I keep all cooking nuts in the freezer. Nuts have lots of oils in them and if stored too long in the pantry, they can get rancid. Nuts keep for at least a year in the freezer. Pecans, walnuts and sliced almonds.

Fruits: If you like to make smoothies, keeping frozen fruits are a good alternative if you don't have fresh on hand. Peaches, strawberries and blue berries.

Meats: I usually have a few freezer bags full of individually frozen chicken breasts (about six). If you like fish, Publix carries a wide variety of frozen fish. A bag of your favorite fish is a good idea. A bag of frozen shrimp is good to have as well, defrost the amount you need and keep the rest in a freezer bag. You can also keep cooked bacon or uncooked bacon in the freezer. I like pepperoni on pizza, so I keep a package of pepperoni frozen and just take out a few pieces when I make pizza.

Puff Pastry: Keep a box of puff pastry in your freezer for all purpose use.

Phyllo Cups: Keep a box of these for quick appetizer needs.

Blue Cheese Biscuit Bites: See this recipe in the recipe section of the book. these biscuits are great to have in the freezer. You can pull out as many as you need for a quick appetizer.

Herbed Chicken Nuggets: See this recipe in the recipe section of the book. Like the blue cheese biscuits, these are great for a quick appetizer.

Frozen Juices: What ever you like, orange juice, limeade, lemonade, pinacolada, strawberry daquiri, etc.

For The Future

I have pointed out a few appliances that are not essential to your kitchen, but would be good to have in the future. I will revisit those as well as adding a few more.

Stand up mixer: This is a wonderful appliance to own if you have the money and room for one. I have found it to be an invaluable tool. The stand up mixer is great to mix things that can be very tedious by hand. Mixers range from 90 dollars to 500 dollars. Hamilton Beach, Sunbeam and Kitchenaid are some of the popular brands. When you are ready for a stand up mixer, shop around and go on line to find the price and brand you are happy with.

Food Processor: A small chopper is a kitchen necessity, but a larger food processor is not needed until you are ready to move on to more elaborate cooking. A good food processor is an excellent thing to have when you start to feel the need for one. I would choose one that has attachments which will allow you to chop, slice and shred.

Deep Fat Fryer: As I said earlier, this product is not for every one, and not needed often. A fryer is a fun thing to have when you want to splurge with calories. I have used mine for fried chicken, shrimp and fish. A fryer is great when you want to make fried appetizers.

Large Crock Pot: At some point a large capacity crock pot can be a good investment.

Miscellaneous: Depending on your life style, likes and needs there are a few other appliances that can be mentioned. Juicer, ice cream maker, rice steamer, bread maker and pasta maker. As you grow in you culinary endeavors, you will know if any of these appliances are desirable.

ORGANIZATION

Kitchen organization is a very important part of cooking. If your kitchen is organized you will feel comfortable, thus able to function in your kitchen effectively. Organization is key. I have learned over the years that an organized kitchen can help you achieve harmony in your over all life. Organizing your kitchen will lead to a good organization in other areas.

Storage: Having good storage products will help you enjoy your kitchen.

Freezer bags: Gallon and quart sizes are wonderful for storing marinating foods, left overs and for freezing foods. I also use freezer bags for all kinds of storage. They don't take up a lot of room when filled.

Plastic containers: I love the new throw away plastic storage options. The containers are inexpensive and come in many wonderful shapes and sizes. You can find these storage containers in grocery, discount and dollar stores. Even though they are disposable, they last for a long time. If you have to take food somewhere that you don't want to worry about taking the dish home, a plastic container is ideal.

Wraps: Every kitchen needs wraps. Plastic cling wrap, wax paper, parchment and a good brand of foil.

Cabinet and Pantry Storage: There are many products on the market today that help organize your cabinets. Wire shelves are good for storing plates. I have wire shelf unit on my pantry door that allows for additional storage of canned goods. I also keep my spices there. Look around at your local hardware store and check out their cabinet storage solutions.

Flatware storage: Drawer inserts are good for organizing your flatware and utensils. These inserts have compartments for different sized items.

Cleaning Products

Keeping your kitchen clean is essential. A clean kitchen is a happy kitchen.

Dishwashing liquid: Buy one that is a grease release. The grease fighter in dishwashing liquid is good to get grease out of clothing.

Dishwasher pellets: I use these instead of the powder.

Scouring powder: Choose one with bleach in it to clean kitchen surfaces. A soft scrub version is good too.

Disinfecting spray: Essential to kill germs and bacteria. Buy one that has bleach.

All purpose spray cleaner: Needed to clean all surfaces.

Scouring pads: I buy the pads with a sponge on one side and a scrubber on the other. My sister cuts hers in half to extend use.

MISCELLANEOUS

Broom: Everyone needs a broom. Chose one that is not too expensive.

Dust pan: I have a dust pan that has a long handle on it so I don't have to bend down to fill it. I bought it at a dollar store.

Trash can: Choose one that will fit under your counter where the sink is or in your pantry (if you have one).

Trash bags: I like the ones that have a draw string. Buy the ones that will fit in your trash can. I like the tall kitchen trash bags. Personally I do not like the scented bags. Buying store brands will save you money.

Dish towels and cloths: Kitchen towels and cloths can be found in most stores; grocery, discount, dollar, department and drug. The ones that match your decor are nice, but are not always absorbant.

Paper towels: I like a strong paper towel. I usually buy a few rolls of good quality and a few of lesser quality. Use the lesser quality towels for jobs that require a lot of towels.

Rubber gloves: I use heavy duty rubber gloves when cleaning.

Small broom: I have a regular size broom but I also have a small hand broom that fits into its own dust pan. The small broom is perfect for little jobs. I found one of these at the dollar store.

Pot scraper: This is a small, flat rubber scraper used to scrape food off of bakeware, cookware and dinnerware.

Household Tools

I am recommending some tools that will be helpful for you to have that do not pertain to the kitchen. I keep some of these tools in my kitchen, so they will be handy for household use.

Screw driver: I have a flat head and a phillips head. I have a very small one and medium one of each.

Measuring tape: A good measuring tape will come in handy for years to come. I have a 25 foot measuring tape, more expensive, but you will use it forever.

Rechargeable electric screwdriver and drill: You will find uses for this for many years to come.

Box cutter: Use with care, but a box cutter is good for many uses.

Hammer: A small one is sufficient for most needs.

Pliers: A small needle nose and small regular pliers.

Safety and Sanitation

There are many things that you will need to consider to keep your kitchen safe and sanitized. I am making suggestions that work for me, but they are not exclusive. There are many other kitchen safety factors. If this is a concern for you, take some time to explore web sites that help with kitchen sanitation.

Knives: Always carry a knife from place to place with the point towards the floor, held down by your side with the blade facing the back. To properly use a knife you should see if you can find an instructional video on line by typing in "knife skills video". Chopping with a knife requires you keep your fingers bent in like a claw. Proper use is something you have to see to understand.

Cutting board: A cutting board is used to chop and slice food. Never use a cutting board to cut meat and then vegetables, fruit or bread. This causes cross contamination. Use the board to cut meats and then spray it with kitchen disinfectant and wash it in the dish washer. Use a separate board to cut vegetables or fruit. Take care to keep cutting boards free of bacteria and contamination. Always place a damp paper towel, dish cloth or rubber liner underneath the board before using. Doing this will keep the board secure while you are using it.

Meat storage: Always store raw meats in the refrigerator, away from raw vegetables and ready -to-eat foods. Keep the meat in a plastic bag in the bottom of your refrigerator.

Cooking poultry: Always cook chicken or turkey to a temperature of 165 degrees. Never serve undercooked poultry.

Unsafe temperature: Bacteria on food will multiply rapidly when left at a temperature between 40 and 140 degrees. Refrigerate leftover food as soon as possible.

Gloves: When handling foods such as poultry or meat I always use rubber gloves. You can purchase these gloves at grocery, dollar and drug stores. They usually come in packages of 10 gloves. I use these gloves constantly at work. You should always wash your hands prior to food preparation but using gloves is added precaution. Gloves are a good thing to use if you are cutting jalapeno peppers or any other kind of hot pepper.

Fire extinguisher: You can find a small fore extinguisher at your local hardware store.

Step Stool: A step stool is a safe way to reach things in your upper cabinets.

Organize Yourself

There are many things you can do to organize yourself. You will find that when you are organized, cooking and entertaining will go smoothly.

Lists: I keep lists when it comes to the kitchen.

- **Grocery list** When you run out of an item, keep a running list for when you make your visit to the store.

- **Entertaining lists** I keep a list of what I need to accomplish each day prior to a dinner or cocktail party. The list includes shopping, setting up, decorating, and serving needs. I know what needs to be done each day prior to a party to make the event go smoothly. Preplanning is key to a fun time for you! When I make my food shopping list I gather my recipes together and list everything I will need for those recipes. I keep the ingredients grouped according to what they are; dairy, produce, meats, canned goods etc. I do my non perishable shopping a week in advance and buy perishables a few days before my party. I decide what foods can be made in advance and get those things done. Trying to do everything at the last minute is no fun! Do as much as you can days before your event. Cleaning, decorating, and choosing serving pieces before hand.

Mis en place: This is a term used in cooking. It means having all the things you will need to prepare a recipe all together prior to starting. Get all your ingredients, utensils and dishes you will need. There is nothing more frustrating then preparing a recipe and having to run around the kitchen for various ingredients. Have them all together and you will have a much more pleasant experience. It is also frustrating if you don't have all your ingredients together and you discover you don't have an ingredient and you have to run to the store (or bribe a friend to do it for you).

Dating: It is helpful to date food when you freeze it. Dating herbs and spice bottles with a permanent marker will help you know how old an item is.

Pantry: I always organize my pantry. I keep canned goods together, baking goods together, dried goods (pastas, rice, etc.) together and snack foods together.

Herbs and spices: In my pantry I group my herbs and spices in a certain way so I can find what I need quickly. All herbs go together (thyme, basil, parsley, oregano, etc.), all sweet spices together (ginger, name, curry powder, ground cloves and ground nutmeg, etc.), all savory spices together (cumin, garlic powder, onion powder, paprika, chili powder, cayenne pepper, ground mustard, etc.) and all seeds together (celery, sesame and poppy, etc.)

HELPFUL TIPS

Through the years I have discovered, by accident or necessity, different tips to make cooking more enjoyable. My tips are what I have found work for me. I am sure there are thousands more out there, but perhaps by reading some of mine, you can come up with some of your own. If you have a particular question you can always go on line and see if you can come up with an answer.

INEXPENSIVE TIPS

Just a few suggestions that I have come up with to help save you money.

Wooden clothes pins: You can buy a bag of these at a discount store for about 1 dollar. I use clothes pins as bag clips. They work great and are very inexpensive.

Baggies: I use baggies fore so many things. Using gallon and quart baggies save space in the pantry, refrigerator and freezer. It is an inexpensive storage solution for many needs beyond your kitchen.

Dried Herbs and spices: The spice isle can offer rather expensive herbs and spices. In my grocery store there is a separate section for a less expensive selection. Some come in plastic canisters, and others are in small bags. For spices and herbs which you will not use often, these small bags are perfect. After opening, store the leftover contents in a snack size zipper bag. Make sure to put the name of the contents on the outside of the bag with a permanent marker. You can also find dried herbs and spices in drug stores. Some will argue that the quality is not as good, but I have no complaints.

Paper plates: I use paper plates whenever possible. You can find inexpensive paper plates and napkins at a dollar store.

Dollar Store:: Check out your local dollar stores and take note of what they carry for future reference. I do not recommend purchasing cleaning products from them unless it is a name brand. I bought a glass cleaner from a true dollar store, and it was watered down.

Coupons Use coupons when ever possible. I don't use them often, but my mom and sister do all the time. The key to using coupons is, use them on things you normally would buy. Do not be lured into buying something just because you have a coupon. Go on line and see if you can find coupons for the products that you buy.

COOKING TIPS

There are so many tips that can help your cooking experience be more productive and comfortable. I have listed but a few, but they are ones that work for me. I hope you find these to be helpful.

Mis en Place: I can not stress this enough. I mentioned it earlier and it is very important. Having everything together before you begin to cook will make your life so much easier!

Clean as you go: If you are preparing more than one dish, try to clean up from one preparation before moving on to another dish. Keeping clean as you go will make your cooking experience less chaotic.

Time management: Calculate how much time you will need to prepare for a meal so you are not rushing at the last minute. Try to do as much in advance as you can.

Recipes: Read through a recipe before you begin to cook. Make sure you have all the ingredients and tools you will need. You also want to make sure you follow the correct sequence for a recipe, and you understand it.

Check dates: Always check expiration dates when buying food, especially dairy. Most stores are diligent about taking away out dated food, but sometimes it does not happen. Always check dates! It is no fun getting home with an item and discovering it is out of date. Even canned goods have expiration dates. Check all dates with your own product at home.

Trash bowl: When preparing meals, keep a bowl close by to use for trash such as peels, trimmed pieces of vegetables, fruits, and meats.

Precooking: Whenever you can, precook certain items prior to preparing a meal. For instance precook a large amount of rice, cool it and keep it in the refrigerator. You can freeze rice for future use and you can also use the rice for a next day meal. Cook spaghetti and store it in the refrigerator. To serve the pasta, run under hot water or heat up in the microwave in a microwave safe container. Pre-brown meats. Precooking when you have the time and storing in the refrigerator will make your life easier. I cook my ground pork a few days before I make my Nam Sod. Always cool your food as quickly as possible and put in the refrigerator as soon as possible. Do not put hot food in your refrigerator, if you do so it will cause the temperature in the refrigerator to rise and could spoil other refrigerated items.

Freezing liquids in a ice cube tray: Freeze liquids such as lemon juice, chicken or beef broth, wine, tomato paste, tomato sauce, etc. in a ice tray. Keep frozen cubes in a freezer bags and use as needed. Each cube is approximately 1 TBSP.

Allowing meats and casseroles to "rest": Meats, such as beef and pork, should rest after cooking in the oven or grill. Resting allows the juices to absorb into the meat. If you cut it right away, all the juices will run out and will cause the meat to be dry. Casseroles are too hot right out of the oven, if you try to cut one immediately, the ingredients will be runny. Letting it rest for 10 minutes will allow it to set and be easier to serve. Rest casseroles and meats on a metal rack, off of the counter surface.

Fresh ginger: I use fresh ginger quite often. To use ginger, peel the skin with a potato peeler. The portion that you do not use, keep the skin on and roll in a damp paper towel and store in a plastic bag.

Puff pastry: I love using puff pastry. I have a section on puff pastry in the recipe portion of this book.

Testing meat for doneness: A few years ago a chef taught me this tip. If you want to ascertain the doneness of beef or pork roast, steak or chicken, test it by poking it with your finger. If it feels like your cheek, it is rare. If it feels like the tip of your nose it is medium. If it feels like your forehead, it is well done.

Burned foods on pots: Sometimes even cooks that have been cooking for years can burn the ingredients in a pot. To get rid of the sticky mess in the bottom of a pot, fill the pot with water and boil for about 10 minutes. The residue should boil out.

Boiling water: To bring water to a boil quickly, put a bit of salt in the water and cover with a lid. Heat on high until the water boils.

Cutting tomatoes: Use a serrated knife to cut tomatoes.

Potatoes: If you precut potatoes for use later, store in cold water to prevent the potatoes from turning brown.

Pre washing: When you buy fruits and vegetables, wash before placing them in the refrigerator. They will be ready to use.

Chicken broth: I use chicken broth to cook rice in, cook vegetables in and make soups out of. I use bouillon cubes for the same purpose.

Boil-in-bag rice: When I need rice quick, I like to use boil-in-bag rice. It is a real time saver.

Cooking liquid: If you cook a vegetable in boiling water, try to save the water to use for soups. The cooking liquid contains vitamins and minerals that have been boiled out of the vegetable. You can also use the cooled liquid to water plants.

Toasting nuts: Pecans, walnuts, pine nuts, almonds and hazelnuts. To toast nuts, preheat your oven to 350 degrees. Spread the nuts on a baking pan lined with parchment paper. Bake the nuts for about 5 minutes and check them. Using a metal spatula redistribute the nuts. Bake for another 5 minutes. Be careful not to burn. Keep a timer on the nuts so you don't forget them. I have done this, and it is a waste of money as nuts are very expensive these days. Cool the nuts before using.

Brown sugar: If your brown sugar has become hard, place some in a microwave safe dish, cover and microwave it for about 15 seconds. The sugar should become soft again.

Spice and herb pairing: I have listed here some foods that pair well with certain herbs and spices. Most spices stay fresh for several months. I must confess that I have some spices that are years old. I don't use them very often. The flavor might not be the absolute best, but they are useable! Herbs stay good about the same. I suggest buying the afore mentioned small spice bags when you only need a small amount.

The one spice I like to keep fresh is ground ginger. It gets a bitter flavor when it is too old.

I have never tried this, but I don't see why you couldn't keep herbs in small freezer bags in the freezer.

Dried herbs and spices

Mexican/Southwest: Chili powder, cumin powder, dried cilantro, oregano, garlic powder, paprika.

Italian: Oregano, thyme, basil, parsley flakes, crushed rosemary, red pepper flakes, garlic powder.

Oriental: Ground ginger, garlic powder, sesame seed.

Cajun: Cayenne pepper, black pepper, onion powder, garlic powder, parsley flakes, thyme.

Indian Curry powder, tumeric, garlic powder, ginger.

Fresh herbs and spices: Whenever possible, I prefer fresh herbs and spices.

Oriental: Ginger, garlic,

Asian: Cilantro, ginger, garlic.

Italian: Italian parsley, rosemary, thyme, oregano, basil, garlic.

Latin: Cilantro, garlic, lime.

French: Parsley, thyme, rosemary, tarragon, garlic.

Greek: Parsley, oregano, garlic, lemon.

Miscellaneous

Garbage Disposal: Never, and I mean never, put rice, pasta or grits down your disposal! I learned the hard way, when I ran a large amount of cooked rice through my disposal a while back. My washing machine was connected to the drain in the sink and I ran a load of clothes later in the evening. I heard a splashing sound and discovered that my washer had backed up and was overflowing at the drain pipe. I had to have the pipes snaked out, at considerable expense. Learn from my mistake and never put any cooked food that will expand down your disposal. Even though the food is cooked, if it is not flushed all the way through your pipes, it will continue to expand and clog up your pipes.

Another tip for a garbage disposal is do not fill it with food and then run it. Turn on the water, turn on the disposal and let the food run into the disposer a little at a time. If you try to pack it full and then run it, you will cause the disposal to clog. This is especially true of potato and carrot peels.

Fresh Refrigerator and Freezer: Place a box of baking soda in your refrigerator and freezer. The soda absorbs odors. It will keep the contents of your refrigerator and freezer fresh.

EQUIVALENTS MEASURING EQUIVALENTS.

Pinch or dash: 1/16 teaspoon

3 teaspoon: 1 tablespoon

4 tablespoons: ¼ cup

1 cup: 8 fluid ounces

2 cups: one pint; 16 fluid ounces

4 cups: 1 quart; 32 fluid ounces; 2 pints

8 cups: 2 quarts; 64 fluid ounces

4 quarts: 1 gallon; 8 pint

Abbreviations: In my recipes TBSP is tablespoon, tsp is teaspoon.

Leftovers

One of the requests of my sorority girls was innovative use of leftovers. I have a few leftover suggestions. I hope you find them helpful.

Chicken: There are many uses for leftover chicken. Chicken and rice or noodle soup (uses for leftover rice or pasta, carrots, and celery), chicken salad, chicken and rice, chicken Caesar salad, chicken chili, chicken fried rice.

Vegetables: Uncooked vegetables that you have left in your refrigerator. Salad, pasta salad and rice salad. Cooked vegetables can be used in soups and stews.

Green Beans: Leftover beans can be marinated and used on salads, or a side dish for sandwiches. Marinate in balsamic vinaigrette.

Rice: There are many uses for leftover rice. Plain rice can be added to soups, casseroles and stews. You can make fried rice with leftover plain rice. Mix sauteed vegetables with rice and leftover chicken for a quick meal. You can also make a rice salad, much like you would a pasta salad.

Beef: Leftover beef can be cut up small and added to vegetable soup. Beef can be sliced and made into beef stew. If you have leftover steak, slice thin and use on top of salad. Leftover steak makes wonderful sandwiches as well.

Hamburger: Process leftover hamburger meat your food chopper. The processed meat can be used for taco meat or chili. Hand chop hamburger meat and add it to vegetable soup.

Boiled shrimp: Chop leftover shrimp into chunks and use for shrimp salad, shrimp fried rice or shrimp bisque.

Resources

There are a few resources that I use. These resources are the ones that I have found to be the most helpful.

Cookbooks: There are so many cookbooks on the market today. Browse your local bookstore and choose ones that are of interest to you. One book that I highly recommend is not a cookbook, but a book of culinary terms. _The New Food Lover's Companion_ has a list of all culinary terms that you should ever need to know. It is handy to have when you have a question on a term, ingredient, technique or dish.

Internet: I have found the internet to be an invaluable tool when searching for recipes. You can simply type in a request and come up with many different sites to explore. You can also find videos on the internet which help you learn proper techniques. Some of my favorite web sites are listed below.

- southernliving.com
- foodnetwork.com
- epicurious.com
- cooksillustrated.com This is a wonderful magazine. The magazine explains cooking techniques, explains which techniques are most effective and compares different products. This magazine would be a worthwhile subscription at some point.

RECIPES

Most of my recipes have been developed over the years. Some are completely my own and others began as a recipe from a book or magazine, but I have changed them to suit myself. Most of the recipes I have in this book are ones the sorority girls have asked for. A few are ones that I have made over the years that are tried and true.

The main thing I want you to know is cooking is not an exact science. It should be fun and stress free. There is no true right or wrong, it is what is right and good for your personal tastes. Not everyone likes to cook, but with the recipes I have included here, you should have no trouble creating enjoyable meals for yourself and others. The key to good cooking is not always in the actual cooking, but in the preparation for cooking; having yourself organized.

I did not always enjoy cooking. When I was newly married, I knew how to cook a few things. I prepared a lot of spaghetti sauce. For my first dinner party I served French Herb Chicken, brown rice and lesueur peas. Thirty years ago it was an elegant meal. Today I know what I served was Coq a vin, which **is** an elegant French chicken dish. My second real dinner party was about 7 years later. I decided to be bold and serve stuffed breast of veal. Ha, try finding a breast of veal 23 years ago. I finally found one, or what would pass as one. The stuffing called for fresh basil leaves and mint. Good thing I planned this meal weeks in advance, fresh basil and mint were not found in grocery stores at that time. I bought a basil plant and mint plant at the garden shop and planted them in my flower garden. Let me tell you, never plant mint in anything other than a pot or confined space! I had mint growing in my grass. I ended up having enough basil and mint for the meal and all was good. I suppose I learned from that early experience that preplanning is the key to low stress cooking.

When you are deciding on what to cook, keep in mind what the finished plate will look like. I have always said that a meal should taste good and look good. Try to avoid a plate that has similar colors and textures. If you are serving chicken, pair it with a green vegetable and a colorful rice pilaf. Beef goes well with orange and green vegetables such as broccoli, carrots, green beans and asparagus. Do not make chicken and serve it with corn and mashed potatoes, not a pretty presentation. Even if you are just cooking for yourself, food should look pleasing. Arrange the food in a pleasing way on the plate. I think of cooking as an art and feel it should look as good as it tastes.

I hope you are able to use some of the recipes that I have put in the book. Where ever possible, I have made suggestions to make a recipe easier for you.

APPETIZERS

The definition of appetizer is any small, bite sized food served before a meal. It can also be a first course served before a meal.

Appetizers are good for a cocktail party, small informal gatherings, tailgating or parties where you take an appetizer to another location.

I have included some easy and fun appetizers. See the section on phyllo cups and puff pastry for additional appetizer ideas. Some appetizers can also be used as main courses when teamed with a nice salad.

HOT ARTICHOKE SPINACH DIP

The bread in this dip is important to help absorb the oils from the cheese and mayonnaise. This is not a low calorie dish, so make it only when you want to splurge.

1	13 oz can artichoke quarters, drained and chopped fine
10	oz package frozen, chopped spinach, thawed and squeezed dry (squeeze with cheese cloth)
1	cup mayonnaise
1	TBSP chopped garlic
1	cup fresh grated Parmesan cheese
2	cups shredded sharp Cheddar cheese, Monterey Jack or Colby Jack
1 ½	cups fresh bread crumbs (white bread, French bread)

Mix all ingredients together in a large bowl. Transfer to a baking dish. Can be made to this point one day in advance, kept covered in the refrigerator. Bring to room temperature. Can be sprinkled with some cheese and baked in the oven 350 for 15 - 20 minutes.

Serve with crackers, sliced French bread, pita chips or bagel chips.

For a fancy presentation, prepare the dip inside a hollowed out round bread loaf. Use the bread that is removed for the bread crumbs. Crumbs can be made by using a food chopper or processor.

Black Bean Salsa

1	14 oz can black beans, drained and rinsed rinse to remove all the cooking liquid)
1	cup frozen corn kernels, thawed
1	cup diced green peppers
1	cup diced onion (red or yellow)
1	14 oz can rotell tomatoes or petite diced tomatoes with chilies
1	tsp chopped garlic
1	tsp ground cumin
½	cup fresh lime juice (use bottled if you have to)
2	TBSP chopped cilantro
1	TBSP apple cider vinegar (optional)
	Diced fresh jalapeno (optional)

Mix all ingredients together except the cilantro. Cover and keep in the refrigerator until ready to serve. Stir in the cilantro before serving. Salsa can be served cold or at room temperature. Serve with *Frito* scoops or tortilla chips.

BLUE CHEESE BISCUIT BITES

This is an awesome appetizer. I have never found anyone who does not love these little biscuits. Even if you don't like blue cheese, I bet you'll like these. My mom first made these for me, and I have loved them ever since. They are easy and keep well in the freezer after baking. Keep a gallon sized freezer bag full in your freezer and pull out a bunch when ever you need them.

1   (4 oz) package Blue cheese

1   stick (½ cup) unsalted butter

1   package butter me not biscuits

Preheat the oven to 350 degrees.

Melt the cheese and butter together in a small sauce pan over med low heat. Open the biscuits and separate each biscuit. Cut the biscuits into quarters. (I use scissors) If you have mini muffin pans, use these, otherwise you can use a parchment covered sheet pan. Whisk the blue cheese mixture a bit to blend the cheese and butter, but try to keep it a bit chunky. Spoon a teaspoon full of cheese over each biscuit and bake for about fifteen minutes. Check to make sure they don't get too brown. If you are going to freeze these, take them out before they are too brown, to allow for additional browning when reheating.

Serve warm.
If you do freeze the biscuits, allow to cool and place in a freezer gallon bag.

To reuse, bake the frozen biscuits at 350 degrees for about 10 minutes, or let them come to room temperature before re-baking.

CHEESE SPREAD

I like to call this glorified pimento cheese. This spread is wonderful and keeps in the refrigerator for at least a week. Great for parties and tailgating.

2   cups shredded sharp cheddar (You can buy already shredded in the cheese section. Store brand will do nicely; just make sure to use SHARP)

½   cup mayonnaise

½   cup chopped, toasted pecans

½   cup chopped green onions

½   cup chopped, cooked bacon (You can use ready to use bacon, just reheat in the microwave to crisp up)

       Sprinkle of garlic powder

Mix all ingredients (adding additional mayonnaise if needed). Store in refrigerator for a few hours allowing the flavors to meld. Serve with baguette slices, *Ritz*, *Captain's Wafers* or pita chips.

CORN AND WALNUT ROLL-UPS

This is a favorite every time!

2	(8 oz packages) cream cheese, softened *
2	TBSP lime juice
1	tsp ground cumin
2	cups frozen corn, thawed
1	cup chopped walnuts, toasted ** and cooled
¼	cup chopped green onion
1	package large flour tortillas

With a hand mixer, blend together cream cheese, lime juice and cumin until smooth. Stir in corn, walnuts and green onion. Place one tortilla on a work surface and spread about ¼ cup cheese mixture over the surface of the tortilla. Roll the tortilla tightly up, but not so much so that the cheese mixture squeezes out. (Use slight pressure) Place in a dish seam side down, and repeat with remaining mixture. (You will have tortillas left over.) This makes about 5 tortillas. Keep roll-ups covered in the refrigerator. These can be made 2 days in advance.

To serve, slice off the ends of the roll and slice the roll into 1 inch rounds. Place rounds on a platter and serve with store bought salsa or fresh salsa.

A pretty presentation would be to place a bowl of salsa in the middle of a large round platter and surround the bowl with the roll-ups and garnish with cilantro leaves.

* To soften cream cheese, open the package and remove the cream cheese. Place the cheese in a bowl and, cover with plastic wrap and let sit out for an hour or so. I tried to speed the process one time by putting the cheese in the microwave, but it got too mushy.

** To toast walnuts, buy chopped walnuts and place in a baking dish. Bake the walnuts in a 350 degree oven for about 5-10 minutes. Keep a close watch so the nuts don't burn.

Variations
Add some shredded Monterey Jack cheese to the mixture, maybe about ¼ cup or more.

Add about 1-2 TBSP finely chopped jalapeno if you like a little heat. (Always use gloves when working with jalapeno's!)

HERBED CHICKEN NUGGETS

I have been making these for at least 20 years. It is a favorite at any cocktail party. These can be made 2 months ahead of time and kept in the freezer, unbaked. You can use plain, store bought bread crumbs. I originally used the Parmesan cheese from a can, but I really like to use freshly grated cheese, or use the shredded cheese from the cheese section of the grocery store. If you use the bagged cheese, use a food processor or food chopper to make the cheese very fine.

This takes a while to prepare, but it is well worth the effort, especially if you are going to freeze it.

8	whole boneless, skinless chicken breast
2	cups dry bread crumbs, finely crushed
1	cup Parmesan cheese, grated
2	TBSP dried thyme
2	TBSP dried basil
1	cup melted butter

These directions are if you are going to freeze the chicken. If you are going to bake the chicken right away, omit the wax paper and place the chicken on a sheet pan coated with nonstick spray.

Cut the chicken into 1 ½ inch, bite sized pieces. Mix the bread crumbs, cheese and herbs together. Place the melted butter in a microwave safe dish. Put the bread crumb mixture in another dish. Dip the chicken pieces into the melted butter and then roll in the bread crumbs. Place the chicken in a single layer on a sheet pan lined with wax paper. Repeat with all the chicken, re-melting the butter in the microwave if needed. If you have to make another layer, place another sheet of wax paper on top of the chicken and continue layering the chicken. Cover with plastic wrap and put in the freezer. When the chicken is frozen, place the chicken in a freezer gallon size bag and keep in the freezer. You can pull out as many nuggets you want as you need them.

Bake fresh or frozen nuggets in an oven pre heated to 400 degrees. Bake for 20 minutes.

Serve with honey mustard, warm pizza sauce or ranch dressing. I have provided a home made honey mustard below.

HONEY MUSTARD

¼	cup vegetable oil
⅓	cup dijon mustard
4	TBSP honey
1	TBSP red wine vinegar
1	tsp grated lemon peel

Mix all ingredients. Can be made a few days in advance.

HOT ONION DIP

This dip is amazing and simple.

1	cup mayonnaise
1	cup chopped Vidalia onions (or sweet onion)
1	cup shredded cheese (Swiss, sharp Cheddar or Monterey Jack)

Mix all ingredients, place in a casserole baking dish and bake in a 350 oven for about 30 minutes. Serve with crackers.

Variation Add a can of crab meat or baby shrimp to the mixture before baking.

MEXICAN DIP

I used to make this in my 20's for any party I was attending, it was always a hit.

1	cup sour cream
1	8 oz package cream cheese, softened (open up & place in a dish, cover and keep out several hours to soften)
1	1.25 oz packet taco seasoning
1	cup shredded sharp cheddar, Colby-jack or Monterey jack
1	cup chopped tomatoes
1	small can sliced ripe olives

Mix the cream cheese, sour cream and taco seasoning together in a bowl. Spread the cheese mixture out on to a shallow serving dish. (I used to use a nice plastic dish I had that was the size of a large plate and had a lip). Sprinkle the cheese on evenly. Sprinkle the tomatoes and olives on top. This can be made a few hours in advance, stored in the refrigerator with plastic wrap to cover. Serve with Fritos scoops, tortilla chips or scoops.

Variation Add ¼ cup chopped green onions or rings of jalapeno slices.

Salsa

This is a well blended version that many restaurants seem to serve.

1	32 oz can whole peeled tomatoes
¼	cup chopped green peppers
¼	cup chopped onion
1	tsp chopped garlic
1	TBSP chopped garlic
1	TBSP cilantro leaves
1	TBSP lime juice
	Pinch cumin
	Pinch pepper
1	TBSP chopped jalapeno (optional)

Place all ingredients in a blender and puree well. If you wish to have a chunkier salsa you can add additional chopped green pepper, onion and tomatoes after blending.

Serve with warm chips. To warm chips, place tortilla chips in an oven proof dish and heat at 350 for about 10 minutes.

You can also add a dash of white wine vinegar if you wish.

SHRIMP DIP

2   cans baby shrimp

1   8 oz cream cheese, softened

1   small grated onion (can be hand grated or chopped fine in food chopper)

1   TBSP prepared horseradish

3   TBSP mayonnaise

Salt and pepper to taste

Mix all ingredients together. Refrigerate, covered for a few hours. Serve with crackers.

SPINACH DIP

This dip is on the package of dry soup mixes, but some don't know about how simple it is.

1	packet dry vegetable soup mix
1	(10 oz) package frozen chopped spinach, thawed and squeezed dry (using cheese cloth; see tips)
1	cup sour cream
1	cup mayonnaise
1	tsp curry powder

Mix all ingredients together until well blended. Place in a container, cover and refrigerate for at least 2 hours and up to one day. Serve with *Fritos*, toasted pita chips, bread slices or crackers.

For a decorative serving idea, hollow out a round loaf of bread and use it to serve the dip in. The chunks of bread that you have from hollowing out the loaf can be used to serve with the dip.

VIDALIA ONION SPREAD

This spread is wonderful for warm weather. It is very refreshing and surprisingly delicious. Wonderful for the beach or a picnic.

6	medium Vidalia onions or sweet onions
½	cup cider vinegar
1	cup sugar
2	cups water
½	cup mayonnaise
1	tsp celery salt (or celery seed)

Slice onions paper thin. (Cut the ends off the onion, peel and cut in half length wise. Lay onion half flat side down and slice thin) Mix with water, sugar and vinegar in a plastic container. Refrigerate 3-4 hours.

Drain well. Mix onions with mayonnaise and celery salt. Serve with crackers such as table water or saltines.

Additional uses use on top of a salad, a sandwich condiment, topper for cold chicken breast or salmon.

SALADS AND SANDWICHES

Some of the salads, such as chicken, shrimp and krab, make wonderful sandwiches as well.

At the sorority house, I tried to create wonderful sandwiches and salads that would complement each other. I will list some sandwiches that I will not include the recipe for, but you can find them on line.

CHICKEN SALAD

I have several different chicken salad recipes. I Like to have fun with the recipes. Chicken is so versatile that you can come up with your own recipes. I use fresh chicken breast and cook it myself, but you can use store bought, precooked chicken breast.

Chicken salad makes wonderful wraps and sandwiches. Another good serving idea is to stuff cooked and cooled puff pastry shells with any of the chicken salads.

CHICKEN SALAD WITH GRAPES AND PECANS

2	cups cooked, diced chicken breast
½	cup red grapes, halved
½	cup chopped pecan pieces, toasted
¼	cup chopped green onion (optional)
½	cup mayonnaise

Mix all ingredients together. Add additional mayonnaise if needed. Store in the refrigerator.

ORIENTAL CHICKEN SALAD

2	cups cooked, diced chicken breast
½	cup canned mandarin oranges, drained
¼	cup sliced almonds, toasted
¼	cup chopped green onions
½	cup dressing

Mix all ingredients. Store in the refrigerator.

Dressing mix ¼ cup vegetable oil, ¼ cup rice wine vinegar, 3 TBSP sugar and 1 TBSP sesame seeds together.

Hawaiian Chicken Salad

2	cups cooked, diced chicken breast
½	cup pineapple tidbits
¼	cup chopped macadamia nuts
¼	cup chopped green onions
½	cup dressing

Mix all ingredients. Store in the refrigerator.

Dressing mix ¼ cup vegetable oil, ¼ cup rice wine vinegar, 3 TBSP sugar and 2 tsp poppy seeds together.

Southwest Chicken Salad

2	cups cooked, diced chicken breast
½	cup frozen corn, thawed
¼	cup chopped roasted red pepper (from a jar, or use pimentos)
¼	cup chopped green pepper
¼	cup chopped green onions
¼	cup salsa
¼	cup dressing

Mix all ingredients. Store in the refrigerator.

Dressing mix ¼ cup olive oil, ¼ cup lime juice and 1 TBSP taco seasoning mix together.

PLAIN OL' CHICKEN SALAD

This is a good use for leftover roasted chicken.

2	cups diced chicken meat (white and dark)
½	cup diced celery
⅔	cup mayonnaise

salt and pepper to taste

Mix all ingredients. Store in the refrigerator.

CAESAR CHICKEN SALAD

2	cups cooked, diced chicken breast
½	cup bottled, creamy Caesar salad dressing
¼	cup shredded Parmesan cheese

Mix all ingredients. Excellent filling for a wrap or pita sandwich along with chopped tomatoes and romaine lettuce.

CORNBREAD SALAD

The first time I tasted corn bread salad, I had three helpings. Trust me, this is a sinful concoction! This is a wonderful salad for picnics, tailgating, or covered dish affairs.

1	Package *Jiffy* cornbread mix, cooked per directions in a baking pan, cooled and crumbled (or any cornbread mix, I prefer *Jiffy*)
2	medium tomatoes, medium dice
1	green pepper, medium dice
1	can corn, drained
1	bunch green onions, chopped
1	cup cooked bacon, chopped*
2	cups shredded sharp cheddar cheese
2	cups ranch dip

Mix the corn, tomato, green pepper and green onion together. Reserve about ¼ cup of the vegetable mixture for garnish.

In a clear glass bowl or dish**, put a layer of half the cornbread crumbles. Sprinkle half of the vegetable mixture, half of the bacon on top. Spread half of the ranch mix over the vegetables. Sprinkle half of the cheese over the ranch mix. Repeat with the cornbread, vegetables, bacon ranch mix and cheese. Sprinkle the top with reserved vegetables. Cover and refrigerate for at least 4 hours or overnight.

* You can use precooked bacon, just crisp in the microwave, cool and chop.

** Make sure the dish is large enough to hold the ingredients. You don't have to serve it in a glass dish, it just looks pretty when you can see the layers.

CUCUMBER AND TOMATO SALAD

Light and refreshing. This salad would also be good on top of crisp romaine.

2	cucumbers (English is preferable since they have no seeds. Some cucumbers have very woody seeds, and I will remove them if they are this way)
2	Tomatoes
½	cup cider vinegar
¼	cup vegetable oil
2	TBSP sugar

Peel and chop the cucumber into 1 inch dice. Cut the tomatoes into 1 inch dice. Combine the tomatoes and cucumbers in a plastic container with a lid. Mix the vinegar, oil and sugar together. Whisk to combine. Pour the vinegar mixture over the vegetables. Marinate in the refrigerator a few hours, shaking the container from time to time.

Add some diced or sliced red onion for a variation.

Fruit Salad

The cinnamon in this recipe gives the fruit a surprising kick.

1	(14 oz) can pineapple chunks, drained
2	cups red grapes, cut in half
2	bananas, sliced
1	granny smith apple cut into chunks
½	cup sour cream
1	tsp ground cinnamon

Mix all of the ingredients together in a bowl. Cover and chill until ready to serve.

KRAB SALAD

This salad is made with imitation crab, which is actually fish. You can use real crab if you wish. If you want to use real crab, buy 2 cans of lump crab meat.

2	cups imitation crab (krab), shredded
1	cup shredded cheddar cheese
¼	cup diced celery
2	TBSP finely diced onion
1	tsp lemon juice
1	cup mayonnaise*

Mix all ingredients together. Store in the refrigerator.

*Use ½ cup mayonnaise and ½ cup softened cream cheese instead, this makes a good spread for crackers.

MAKE YOUR OWN PASTA SALAD

This recipe is for the sorority girls that wanted to know different ways to create a pasta salad. Creating a pasta salad is a good way to use leftover ingredients. There is no right or wrong! I am listing numerous ingredients. You can make your own combinations!

1 pound cooked, cooled pasta (penne, rotini, bow tie, orzo, shells)

1 cup of any of the following

  peeled and cubed cucumber

  cubed carrot

  grape tomatoes, halved

  broccoli, cut into small pieces

  ripe olives

  chopped celery

  pepperoni

  cubed mozzarella cheese

  crumbled feta cheese

  artichoke hearts, chopped

  chopped green, red or yellow peppers

  steamed asparagus, cut into small pieces

  sliced mushrooms

Mix all your ingredients and toss the pasta with one of the dressings I have included in this book, or a bottled dressing.

NAM SOD (THAI PORK OR CHICKEN SALAD)

This is a wonderful Thai salad. I make this quite often, as it is refreshing, filling and low fat. Ground pork is very lean.

1	pound ground pork or chicken
½	cup chopped green onion
½	cup finely sliced red onion
1	TBSP red pepper flakes, or to taste (optional)
1	cup dry roasted peanuts
2	TBSP chopped, fresh cilantro

Cook the meat on a pot of boiling water. Lower heat and simmer until cooked, about 10 minutes, breaking up large chunks. Drain meat in a colander. Cool and crumble into a mixing bowl. Mix in sauce, green onions, red onions and red pepper flakes. Cover and chill until ready to serve.

To serve I like to finely shred napa cabbage or lettuce and place about 1 cup on a plate. I put about 1 cup of the meat on top of the cabbage, sprinkle with ¼ cup of peanuts and 2 tsp cilantro. I like to have shredded carrot (store bought in a bag) and sliced radishes on the side. I like to serve Asian marinated cucumber slices with this dish.

SAUCE

¼	cup lime juice
2	TBSP rice wine vinegar
1	tsp fish sauce (optional)*
½	tsp salt
1	tsp ground lemon grass**

Whisk all ingredients in a small bowl.

* Found in the oriental section of your grocery store. Also called Nampla. It is used in many Asian and Thai dishes. It is stinky, so be forewarned.

** I buy the tube of ground lemon grass in the produce section of my grocery store.

CRUNCHY ORIENTAL CHICKEN SALAD

Years ago I lived in Atlanta and played a lot of tennis. Tennis in Atlanta is as much about the food as it is about the tennis. This salad was served to my team and we all demanded the recipe. It is a real winner!

3	cups cooked, chopped chicken breast
4	green onions, sliced
1	package ramen noodles, crushed
1	cup sliced almonds, toasted
2	cups thinly sliced napa cabbage

Mix all of the above ingredients and toss with the following dressing. Allow to sit in the refrigerator several hours or over night.

DRESSING

1	cup vegetable oil
6	TBSP rice wine vinegar
2	tsp salt
3	TBSP sugar

Mix well and pour over the noodle mixture.

Patti's Salad

Strange ingredients, but a wonderful salad.

1	bag chopped romaine
1	packet good seasons dry dressing mix (using directions on the package, but use with balsamic vinegar and olive oil)
1	jar marinated artichokes, chopped
2	TBSP toasted sesame seeds
¼	cup toasted, slivered almonds
½	cups shredded parmesan cheese

Add the artichokes to the dressing mix. Mix the dressing mix with the romaine. Sprinkle the cheese, sesame seeds & almonds on top. Toss to mix and serve.

SHRIMP SALAD

¼	pound cooked, peeled shrimp
½	cup mayonnaise
¼	cup ketchup
¼	cup diced celery
1	tsp lemon juice

salt and pepper to taste

Chop the shrimp and add all the other ingredients. Mix well. Keep refrigerated until ready to use.

Serve as a salad by itself.

Serve as a sandwich with lettuce and tomato using a roll , bun, croissant, pita or wrap.

SPINACH SALAD WITH POPPY SEED DRESSING

I have made this at the sorority house and it is always a favorite! This recipe serves two people.

½   bag fresh baby spinach, long stems pinched off

5   strawberries, sliced

1   hard boiled egg, chopped

¼   cup chopped, cooked bacon*

¼   cup sliced almonds, toasted

2   green onions, chopped (optional)

¼   cup poppy seed dressing

Toss the spinach with the dressing in a large bowl. Place some of the spinach on a small plate. Sprinkle with the bacon, egg, almonds, strawberries and onion.

* You can use precooked bacon from the grocery store, just crisp the bacon in the microwave and chop it after it has cooled. Do not use immitation bacon bits.

POPPY SEED DRESSING

2   TBSP red wine vinegar

1   TBSP vegetable oil

1   TBSP granulated sugar

2   tsp poppy seeds

Mix the vinegar, oil and sugar together and whisk until the sugar is incorporated, add the poppy seeds and serve. If you make the dressing in advance, store in the refrigerator. Whisk well before using on the salad.

STACIE'S MEDITERRANEAN SALAD

My friend Stacie made this salad when a group of women stayed in Destin Beach one year. It is a wonderful and refreshing salad. This salad is great for a crowd. To make it for less, simply cut the recipe in half.

2	heads chopped romaine or 2 bags chopped romaine
1	cucumber, peeled, cut in half length wise and sliced
2	cups grape tomatoes
½	pound fresh green beans, blanched and cooled
8	ounces crumbled Feta cheese
1	bottle *Newman's Own Caesar Salad Dressing*, drain off the oil

Put the romaine in a large bowl and toss with the dressing. Add the cucumbers, tomatoes, green beans and cheese. Toss and serve.

Sweet & Sour Slaw

This slaw marinates overnight and is a wonderful side dish for seafood and Caribbean style meals.

1	head cabbage, finely sliced. (You can find angel hair cabbage, in bags, in the produce section. Buy 2-3 bags
1	cup diced onion
1	cup diced green pepper
1	cup granulated sugar

Place the cabbage in a large container. Sprinkle the onions and green peppers over the top. Evenly pour the sugar on top of the vegetables. Pour the following dressing over top, cover and chill overnight in the refrigerator. (Do not stir)

To serve, mix well. Keeps in the refrigerator for a week.

Dressing

½	cup cider vinegar
¼	cup vegetable oil
2	tsp ground mustard
2	tsp celery seed

Put all ingredients in a sauce pan and bring to a boil. Allow to cool slightly before pouring it over the cabbage.

TUNA PASTA SALAD

I developed this pasta salad 8 or 9 years ago. I don't know if it is unique, but every one that has it seems to love it. I was fortunate enough to have it published in the Columbia State paper about 3 years ago. It is a great salad to have on hand for vacations at the beach, picnics and tailgating. You can cut this recipe by half or you can omit the pasta to make a good tuna salad for sandwiches.

1	Large can solid white tuna, drained and flaked
1	Box (1 lb.) bow tie pasta, cooked, drained, rinsed and cooled
8	Green onions, chopped
1	cup raisins
1	cup toasted and chopped pecans
¼	tsp ground ginger
½	tsp curry powder
1	TBSP fresh lemon juice (use bottled as an alternative)
½	cup mayonnaise
½	reduced fat sour cream

Mix tuna, raisins, ginger powder, curry powder, green onions and lemon juice together in a large bowl. Stir in the mayonnaise and sour cream. Add the pasta and mix well. Cover and store in the refrigerator. To serve, add more mayonnaise if to dry.

TUNA SALAD

This is my daughters favorite tuna salad.

1	large can solid white tuna, drained
½	cup mayonnaise
½	tsp ground ginger
¼	tsp curry powder
2	tsp lemon juice

Mix all ingredients.

Additions ¼ cup of any of the following diced onion, chopped egg, diced celery or 12 TBSP pickle relish.

WRAPS

You can use flour tortillas as a wrap for so many different fillings. It can be a quick snack or lunch. I have listed some fillings for wraps, but really, anything goes. Just about anything you can do with a sandwich, you can make into a wrap This also works for pita's. Cut the pita in half, open it up and fill with any of the following..

SALAD WRAPS

Any of the salads I have included in this book; Chicken, Krab, Tuna, Shrimp or Egg salad. Add lettuce and roll up into a wrap.

Caesar Salad with chicken and chopped tomatoes.

Turkey or Ham with cheese, lettuce, tomato, mayonnaise, mustard, cucumber, green pepper, sprouts.

Mexican Wrap: Chicken breast mixed with Mexican dressing (see recipe), black beans, corn, tomatoes and lettuce.

Veggie Wraps: What you have in the refrigerator broccoli, celery, cucumbers, green peppers, tomatoes, etc. Slice and mix with your favorite dressing and wrap it up!

Simply use your imagination and create what you like.

GRILLED CHEESE AND BEYOND

The sorority girls love grilled cheese. At one time I made them every Wednesday. I had to cut it down to once a month, I was making about 120 grilled cheeses during lunch. It is a wonderfully comforting food. It is so easy to make, but the key is not to burn it.

For 4 Grilled cheeses, using a square griddle (see cookware)

8	pieces white or wheat bread
8	slices american cheese
2	TBSP melted butter

Put 2 slices of cheese between 2 slices of bread. Heat the griddle on med-low. Add 1 TBSP melted butter and brush over the entire surface of the griddle. Place the bread in the pan. Grill for about 5 minutes, checking for browning. Brush the top of the bread with the butter (using more butter if needed). Flip the grilled cheese once the bottom is brown. Grill the other side until brown. Remove for pan and eat immediately.

Variations Add the following ingredients before grilling
Cooked Bacon

Ham

Tomato

Pickle chips

Turkey

Mustard

Mayonnaise

*If you want to make just one grilled cheese, melt 1 tsp of butter in a sauté pan, grill as directed, lift the grilled cheese from the pan, add 1 tsp butter, allow to melt and flip the grilled cheese.

Mini Hawaiian Sandwiches

This sandwich is good for picnics and tailgating.

1	package Hawaiian rolls
1	(4 ounce) package cream cheese, softened
1	(8 0unce) can crushed pineapple
1	package shaved ham

Slice the rolls in half. Melt 1 TBSP butter in a griddle. Grill the cut side of the rolls until brown. Drain the pineapple and sauté in a pan on high heat, 10 minutes, stirring frequently. Open the ham and heat in the microwave 1 minute. Spread 2 TBSP cream cheese on each of the rolls, place a few slices of the ham on top, followed with 2 TBSP grilled pineapple. Put the top on the roll. Serve immediately or keep covered in the refrigerator. Re-heat in the microwave to serve. If you are using it for tailgating, serve cold.

Sandwiches

Cuban Sandwich

Grilled Chicken Sandwich with pesto and feta cheese

Muffalatas

Shrimp Po Boys

Reubens

Meatball subs

Soups and Sauces

I love Soup. I can have soup any time of the year even though some are more suited to a certain season. I think soup is the ultimate comfort food. There is no right or wrong with soup. You can add to the pot what you like and come up with a wonderful creation.

The sauces are mostly cold sauces such as cocktail and tartar.

CREAM OF TOMATO SOUP

A good friend of mine first made this soup for me about 10 years ago. I loved it and have adapted it for my own use. The girls at the sorority love this soup served with grilled cheese.

1	(32 ounce) can whole peeled tomatoes
1	cup water
2	chicken bouillon cubes
3	garlic cloves
1	medium onion, peeled and quartered
½	stick butter
1	TBSP dried basil
1	cup Half & Half

Put all ingredients except the half & half, in a large pot. Bring to a boil, lower temperature, cover and simmer for about 20 minutes. Remove for heat, take off cover and allow to cool. When the tomato mixture is close to room temperature, puree in batches using a blender*. Pour back into a pot. Add the half & half and reheat, do not boil.

* Do not puree while the mixture is hot. The heat will cause steam expansion and will pop the top off of the blender. Dangerous and messy!

CREAM SOUP BASE

Start with this base and add different ingredients to create various soups.

6	TBSP butter
6	TBSP flour
2	cups chicken broth
2	cups half & half
½	cup white wine

Melt butter in sauté pan. Whisk in flour and cook over med-low heat for 5 minutes. Remove from heat. In a 4 quart sauce pan heat the chicken broth, half and half to almost boiling. Add the flour mixture to the liquid (use a rubber spatula to scrape all the flour mixture into the liquid). Whisk until the mixture becomes thick.

Remove from heat and use or store in the refrigerator for one week or the freezer for one month.

BROCCOLI

Cook 2 cups broccoli florets in boiling, salted water until tender. Sauté ¼ cup onion in a small sauté pan until the onion is translucent. Drain the broccoli and reserve ½ cup. Add the broccoli and onion to the cream base. Puree in batches in a blender. Put the puree mixture in a soup pot and heat on low. Chop reserved broccoli and add to the soup.

Variation add ½ cup shredded sharp cheddar cheese for a cream of broccoli and cheese soup. Add some chicken broth if the soup is too thick.

ASPARAGUS

1 bunch asparagus, trimmed and cut into 2 inch pieces. Simmer asparagus in salted water until tender. Drain asparagus, reserving ¼ cup. Add asparagus to cream base and puree in batches in blender. Put the puree mixture in a soup pot and heat on low. Ladle into soup bowls and garnish with a few pieces of reserved asparagus.

MUSHROOM

Sauté 2 cups sliced mushrooms in 1 TBSP butter. Add to the cream mixture and puree in batches in a blender. Put puree mixture in a soup pot and heat over low heat.

SHRIMP AND CORN

1	cup peeled, cooked shrimp, chopped
1	cup frozen corn, thawed
½	cup cooked, diced carrot
1	tsp parsley flakes

salt to taste

Add all ingredients to the cream base and heat in a soup pot over low heat.

Garnish soup bowls with chopped, fresh parsley.

Roasted Red Pepper

add ½ cup chopped roasted red pepper from a jar to the cream soup base. Puree in batches in blender. Heat in a soup pot over low heat. Garnish soup with diced roasted red pepper.

Cheddar Ale

Omit the wine in the base and use ½ cup beer. Add 1 cup shredded sharp yellow or white cheddar cheese. Heat in a soup pot over low heat. Garnish with shredded cheese

Celery

2	cups chopped celery
2	TBSP diced onion

Sauté celery and onion in 1 TBSP butter for about 10 minutes. Add to the cream base and puree in batches in a blender. Put puree mixture in a soup pot and heat over low heat. Garnish with a celery leaf or crouton.

Carrot

1	cup diced carrot
2	TBSP diced onion

Cook carrot in salted water until it is tender. Sauté the onion in a small pan for about 5 minutes. Add the carrot and onion to the cream base. Add 1 tsp ground ginger. Puree the mixture in batches. Heat in a soup pot over low heat. Garnish with croutons.

CRAB AND GREEN ONION

½   cup chopped green onion

1   tsp minced garlic

1   TBSP butter

½   pound fresh crab meat or 1 can jumbo lump crab meat
      (drained)

Sauté the onion and garlic in the butter 5 minutes on medium low
heat. Stir into the cream base and add the crab. Heat slowly and serve
in bowls garnished with ½ tsp chopped green onion.

Variation Add ½ cup shredded cheddar to the soup before warming.

GAZPACHO

I can eat a gallon of gazpacho. This is a quick and easy recipe.

3	cups V8 juice or tomato juice
½	cup chopped tomato
½	cup peeled, chopped cucumber
½	cup diced celery
¼	cup diced green pepper
2	TBSP chopped green onion
¼	tsp ground pepper
1	tsp lemon juice
2	tsp rice vinegar
	dash tabasco (optional)
1	TBSP finely chopped jalapeno pepper (optional)

Mix all the ingredients in a bowl. Transfer to a plastic container with a lid and store in the refrigerator. I like to put a spoon full of sour cream in my bowl of gazpacho.

MINESTRONE

1	TBSP olive oil
1	TBSP chopped garlic
½	cup diced celery
1	cup diced onion
1	cup chopped zucchini
1	cup chopped cabbage
1	(32 ounce) carton chicken broth
1	(15 ounce) can Italian style green beans
1	(15 ounce) can drained kidney beans
1	(15 ounce) can diced tomatoes, drained
2	cups cooked elbow macaroni or other small pasta
1	tsp dried oregano
1	tsp dried basil
	grated parmesan cheese

In a large dutch oven or soup pot heat the oil over medium heat. Add the onion and sauté 5 minutes. Add the garlic and sauté 2 minutes more. Add the celery and cabbage and cook a few more minutes. Add all other ingredients except the pasta and cheese. Cover and simmer 1 hour. Add the pasta and simmer 10 minutes. Serve in soup bowls and garnish with the cheese.

Taco Soup

3	cups chicken broth
1	cup diced, cooked chicken
1	cup black beans (rinsed & drained)
1	cup frozen corn
1	can petite cut tomatoes
1	cup onions, chopped
1	TBSP chopped garlic
2	cups cooked rice (or left over Mexican rice)
1	tsp ground cumin
2	tsp chili powder
2	tsp dried cilantro or 1 TBSP chopped fresh cilantro
2	TBSP taco seasoning

Crushed tortilla chips for garnish

Sauté the onion and garlic in 1 TBSP olive oil in a large pot for 5 minutes. Add all other ingredients (except crushed chips) and simmer for 15 minutes. Spoon into bowls and garnish with crushed tortilla chips. Sprinkle shredded cheddar or monterey jack cheese on top and a dollop of sour cream if desired.

Vegetable Soup

I have been making this soup for years. It is wonderful on a cold winter day served with cornbread and a salad.

1   (32 ounce) can tomato sauce

1   (14 OUNCE) can chicken broth

1   (10 ½ ounce) can beef broth

1   bag mixed vegetables (peas, corn, carrots and beans)

1   baking potato, peeled and finely diced

1   tsp dried basil

Mix all ingredients in a large soup pot, cover and simmer one hour, stirring frequently.

Variations Add any of the following to the soup.

1   cup chopped celery

2   cups finely shredded cabbage

1   cup sliced okra

1   cup cooked hamburger meat

1   cup leftover beef, diced

1   cup diced onion

1   cup diced, cooked ham

WHITE CHICKEN CHILI

A favorite of my son and the sorority.

4	cups cooked chicken breast, diced
2	(15 ounce) cans great northern beans
1	(15 ounce) can cannelloni beans
2	(4 ounce) chopped green chilies
1	(32 ounce) carton chicken broth
1	cup half & half
½	cup white wine
½	tsp cumin powder
½	tsp oregano
2	cups shredded Monterey Jack cheese

Mix all ingredients except for the cheese in a large soup pot. Simmer for 30 minutes. Add the cheese and cook an additional 15 minutes, stirring frequently.

Barbeque Sauce

There are thousands of barbeque sauces. I have a few that are my favorites. All of these can be used on any meat; chicken, beef, pork. You can bake or grill the meat.

Sauces can be stored in your refrigerator (if not all used) for about a month.

South Carolina BBQ Sauce

⅔	cup yellow, prepared mustard
½	cup granulated sugar
1	cup cider vinegar
2	TBSP chili powder
1	tsp red pepper flakes
½	tsp soy sauce
2	TBSP butter

Put all ingredients in a sauce pan and simmer foe about 10 minutes.

Southwest BBQ Sauce

2	TBSP garlic, chopped
¼	cup chopped onion
2	cups ketchup
½	cup water
½	cup brown sugar
3	TBSP butter
½	cup Worcestershire sauce
¼	cup cider vinegar
3	TBSP chili powder
2	tsp instant coffee granules
¼	tsp ground cloves

Melt the butter and saute the garlic and onion in a sauce pan for about 5 minutes. Add all other ingredients and simmer 15 minutes. Remove from heat and allow to cool put the sauce in a blender and process until smooth.

Bourbon BBQ Sauce

I buy a mini bottle of bourbon to make this sauce. This is a wonderful sauce for baby back ribs and salmon.

½	cup brown sugar
¼	cup soy sauce
¼	cup ketchup
¼	cup bourbon
2	TBSP butter

Put all ingredients in a sauce pan and simmer for about 10 minutes.

Simple BBQ Sauce

My mom has been using this sauce for years to cook rump roast.

1	cup ketchup
¼	cup Worcestershire sauce
2	TBSP garlic powder

Mix all ingredients.

Versatile Barbeque Sauce

I call it this because you can add different ingredients to develop a sauce suited to your theme.

1	cup Ketchup
½	cup rice wine vinegar
½	cup brown sugar
2	TBSP lemon juice
¼	cup butter
1	TBSP garlic
2	TBSP chopped onion
1	TBSP Worcestershire sauce
1	TBSP soy sauce
2	TBSP dijon mustard

Simmer all ingredients in a sauce pan for 20 minutes. Cool sauce and puree in blender.

To personalize this sauce add the following ingredients before pureeing:

CARIBBEAN SAUCE

½	cup mango
12	tsp jalapeno pepper
2	TBSP cilantro
2	TBSP lime juice
1	tsp cumin

HAWAIIAN SAUCE

| ½ | cup crushed pineapple |
| 2 | TBSP chopped green pepper |

ORANGE SAUCE

| ½ | cup orange marmalade |
| 2 | TBSP chopped green onion |

ORIENTAL SAUCE

½	cup plum sauce
2	TBSP chopped green onion
2	tsp ground ginger

Cocktail Sauce

1   cup ketchup

1-3   TBSP prepared horseradish (depending on your taste)

1   tsp lemon juice

       dash pepper

Mix all ingredients together. Chill and serve with boiled shrimp, steamed oysters or a shrimp po boy sandwich.

Tartar Sauce

1	cup mayonnaise
1	tsp sugar melted with 2 tsp white vinegar
2	TBSP sweet pickle relish
	dash garlic powder
½	tsp lemon juice

Mix all ingredients. Serve with shrimp, fish, scallops, or oysters.

HORSERADISH SAUCE

Good with steak and roast beef sandwiches.

¼   cup mayonnaise

¼   cup sour cream

1-2   TBSP prepared horseradish

Mix all ingredients. Keep in a container in the refrigerator.

Mock Hollandaise Sauce

Good on steamed broccoli and asparagus.

1   cup mayonnaise

2   TBSP lemon juice

Mix ingredients well. Keep in a container in the refrigerator.

WHITE SAUCE

½   cup mayonnaise

½   TBSP ground ginger (or fresh from a tube)

½   tsp. paprika

½   tsp. garlic powder

2   TBSP sugar melted with ¼ cup white vinegar

Mix the mayonnaise, ginger, garlic and paprika together. Add 1 TBSP vinegar mixture and stir well. Adjust seasonings to taste. This sauce is wonderful on stir fried vegetables and fried rice.

Main Dishes

There are so many wonderful main dishes. I had to limit myself and am including just the ones that I know are easy yet wonderful.

Chicken Bog

This dish is a specialty of the piedmont area of South Carolina. You can't go to a piedmont Baptist church dinner with out having Chicken Bog. I call it the Jambalaya of South Carolina. It is basically a chicken and rice dish with a twist.

1   whole baking hen

1   small onion, quartered

2   celery stalks

3   cups white rice

1   package smoked sausage

2   TBSP ground pepper

2   tsp salt

6   cups chicken broth (from the cooking liquid)

Put the chicken in a soup pot. Fill with enough water to cover the hen. Add the onion and celery. Bring to a slow simmer and cook, covered 1 ½ hour. Remove the hen from the broth and allow the hen and broth to cool. Strain the broth into a sauce pan. Measure out 6 cups. If there is not enough liquid, add enough canned chicken broth to make 6 cups. If you have more than 6 cups reserve the extra in the refrigerator for another use, or freeze it.

When the chicken is cool enough to handle, pull the meat from the bone and remove the skin. Use gloves rubber gloves when doing this. Put the meat in a dutch oven. Cut the sausage into ½ slices. Add the sausage to the dutch oven. Put the 3 cups rice in with the chicken and sausage. Add the chicken broth. Bring the pot to a boil on the stove top. Put on the lid and bake in a 350 degree oven for 1 hour. Stir the rice mixture to combine all ingredients in the pot. Sprinkle the pepper and salt over the rice and stir well.

Serve with corn bread and southern style green beans.

Quick Version Use a store bought, cooked chicken. Take the meat from the bone. Use 6 cups store bought chicken broth.

Chicken Cordon Bleu in Puff Pastry

1	puff pastry sheet, thawed
4	skinless, boneless chicken breast
1	TBSP olive oil
1	TBSP butter
4	slices Swiss cheese
4	sliced cooked ham
1	egg beaten with 1 TBSP water (egg wash)

Heat the oil and butter in a sauté pan and cook the chicken, browning on both sides. Put chicken on a paper towel lined plate, cover with plastic wrap and chill in the refrigerator 1 hour and up to 24 hours.

Roll out the pastry sheet, on a lightly floured work surface, into a 14 inch square. Cut the square into 4 equal pieces. Place 1 slice of Swiss cheese in the middle of each pastry. Top with the ham, cutting to fit if needed. Place one piece of chicken on each square. Brush the edges of the pastry with the egg wash. Fold the pastry up over the chicken overlapping ends and sealing. Place each pastry on a parchment lined sheet pan, seam side down. Brush the pastry with the egg wash. Bake in a 400 degree oven for 25 minutes until golden.

Filet Mignon with Blackberry-Balsamic Sauce

A wonderful and quick meal. This is a good company or date dish.

Sauce

½   cup balsamic vinegar

2   TBSP blackberry jelly (not jam)

2   TBSP Butter

Reduce the balsamic vinegar in a sauce pan for about 5 minutes, or more, until thickened and reduced by half. Lower heat and add the blackberry jelly, whisking until the jelly is melted. Add the butter and whisk until melted and incorporated.

Serve the sauce by spooning ½ on a filet mignon.

Filet Mignon

2   filet Mignon slices, about 1 ½ inches thick

Heat 1 TBSP olive oil in a sauté pan on med-high heat. Sauté the steaks about 7 minutes on each side for rare. Place one piece of mignon on a plate. Drizzle with the warm sauce and serve with side items of your choice. (I have made some side item suggestions in the menu pairing section).

Variation Add 2 TBSP crumbled blue cheese on top of the filet after spooning the sauce on.

French Herb Chicken

A wonderful chicken dish that is traditionally called Coq a Vin.

1	whole chicken, cut into pieces (or you can buy 4 chicken breasts and 4 chicken legs or thighs, skin on)
2	TBSP chopped garlic
2	cups dices carrots
2	cups sliced mushrooms
2	cups red wine*
4	cloves
2	bay leaves
2	pepper corns
2	TBSP butter
2	TBSP vegetable oil
½	cup flour

Dredge chicken pieces in the flour. Brown in oil in a large sauté or fryer pan (do in batches if you need to), over med-high heat. Remove chicken and add the butter. Add the bay leaves, cloves and pepper corns. Cook for 2 minutes. Add the garlic and cook another 2 minutes. Add the carrots and mushrooms and cook 5 minutes. Add the wine and simmer 10 minutes. Place the chicken in a dutch oven or large covered baking dish. Pour the wine and vegetable mixture over top of chicken. Bake at 375 degrees for 1 hour. Discard the bay leaves and serve. This dish goes well with brown rice and Leseuer peas.

* Some people say to use wine that you would drink, but I usually purchase inexpensive red wine and store the leftover in the pantry or refrigerator. I find inexpensive wine in this dish is just fine. Of course, you can buy a nice wine and drink the remainder with dinner.

HAM, BROCCOLI & CHEESE PUFF PASTRY ROLL

I would serve this for lunch with a nice salad.

1	sheet puff pastry, thawed
½	pound sliced, cooked ham*
4	ounces cream cheese, softened
½	cup shredded sharp cheddar
¼	cup finely diced onion
½	cup chopped, frozen broccoli, thawed
1	egg slightly beaten with 1 TBSP water.

Unfold the pastry and put on a lightly floured work surface. Roll into a 12 x 16 inch rectangle. Have the short end facing you.

Mix the cream cheese, cheddar cheese and onion together. Spread the cream cheese mixture over the pastry to within 1 inch all the way around except leaving about a 3 inch edge on the end away from you. Sprinkle the broccoli on top of the cream cheese and then layer with the ham. Brush the 3 inch lip with egg wash. Roll up jelly-roll style. Place the roll on a parchment lined sheet pan, seam side down. Stretch the ends down and tuck them under. Brush the pastry with the egg wash.

Bake in a 400 degree oven for 25 minutes until golden brown. Remove from oven and let rest about 10 minutes. Slice into 4 inch pieces and serve.

* You can use turkey, or both.

A nice addition to this would be ¼ cup crumbled, cooked bacon.

HERBED CHICKEN BREAST IN PUFF PASTRY

1	sheet puff pastry, thawed
4	skinless, boneless chicken breasts
1	TBSP olive oil
1	TBSP butter
4	ounces herbed cream cheese spread
4	TBSP shredded mozzarella cheese
1	egg beaten with 1 TBSP water (egg wash)

In a sauté pan heat the oil and butter on med-high heat. Add the chicken breasts and brown on both sides. Remove the chicken from the pan and place on a paper plate lined with paper towels. Cover with plastic wrap and chill in the refrigerator. Chill one hour or up to 24 hours.

Unfold the pastry sheet and roll out to about a 14 inch square on a lightly floured work surface. Cut the pastry into 4 equal squares. Spread ¼ of the cream cheese in the center of each square. Sprinkle 1 TBSP mozzarella on top of the cream cheese. Place 1 chicken breast on top of each square. Brush the edges of the pastry with the egg wash. Bring sides of the pastry up over the chicken and seal. Place the chicken on a parchment lined sheet pan. Brush with egg wash. Bake in a 400 degree oven for 25 minutes until golden brown.

INDIVIDUAL BEEF WELLINGTON

This makes a perfect meal when you want to impress. It looks complicated, but it is really quite easy. Serves 2

2	two inch thick filet mignons
1	puff pastry sheet, thawed
2	TBSP butter
1	cup chopped mushrooms
1	tsp chopped garlic
1	TBSP chopped green onion
1	tsp dried thyme
½	tsp salt
¼	tsp pepper
2	TBSP heavy cream
1	TBSP white wine
1	egg, beaten with 2 tsp water

Sear the beef on each side about 1 minute on each side on high heat.

Place the meat on a paper towel lined plate. Cool and cover with plastic wrap. Keep in the refrigerator. Can be prepared a day in advance.

Sauté the mushrooms in the butter for 5 minutes. Add the garlic, salt, pepper, thyme and sauté 5 minutes more. Add the cream and wine, cooking for 5 minutes on high to reduce the liquid to almost nothing.

Place the puff pastry sheet on a floured work surface. Roll it out slightly and cut in half with a pairing knife. Spoon ½ of the mushroom mixture onto the puff pastry, spreading it to the size of the piece of beef. Place the beef on top of the mushroom mixture. Cut around the beef* leaving 2 inches of pastry all the way around. Brush around the beef with the egg mixture. Bring the pastry up around the beef, stretching to make it meet in the middle. Fold and overlap the sheet around the beef, covering completely, and seal by smoothing the folds down. Place, folded side down, on a baking sheet that has been sprayed with non-stick spray. Repeat with the other half of the pastry, mushroom mixture and beef. Brush the wellington's with the egg mixture (egg wash)**. Bake in the oven at 400 degrees for 15 minutes or until puff pastry is nice and golden brown. Fifteen minutes for rare, longer for more done meat. Allow the wellington to rest 10 minutes before serving. (remember that the beef will continue to cook as it rests.

I have made some side dish suggestions in the menu section.

*To make the wellington extra special use a small cookie cutter on the extra puff pastry and put on top of the wellington after you have brushed it with the egg wash. Brush the addition with egg wash as well. Some of the suggestions for shapes are heart, star, leaf or even circle.

** Wellington can be prepared to this point, and kept covered, in the refrigerator a day in advance.

Low Country Boil

In other parts of the country this would be called a clam bake or crab boil. On the coast of South Carolina and Georgia it is also called Frogmore Stew. Serves 2 people

2	Fresh corn on the cob, broken in half (I like white corn)
1	pound raw shrimp (I prefer peeled, but most boils call for shell on, as part of the fun of the meal is peeling and eating the shrimp. Plus the shells give a good flavor)
1	package smoked sausage, cut into 2" rounds
8	small red new potatoes
1	lemon, cut into quarters
4	cloves garlic
1	can beer (optional)
1	TBSP old bay seasoning

Bring 2 gallons of water to boil in a large soup pot. Add the lemon, garlic, seasoning and beer. Bring to another boil. Add the potatoes and cook 10 minutes. Add the corn and cook another 10 minutes. Add the sausage and cook 5 minutes. Add the shrimp and cook another 10 minutes, or until the shrimp are pink. Spoon out the contents with a slotted spoon or drain in a colander. Serve with lemon wedges and cocktail sauce. The traditional way to serve this stew is to put all the ingredients on news paper covered table (preferably out doors) and give each person a paper plate. This is a wonderful casual meal! Great for the beach.

Marinades For Meats

The marinades I have listed here can be used for most meats, but I have given the most preferable meat in the recipe. Most meats should marinate several hours, up to overnight.

Latin Spice Marinade

Excellent on fresh boneless ham, fish and chicken.

10	peeled garlic clove
2	TBSP fresh thyme leaves
2	TBSP rosemary leaves
8	fresh basil leaves
¼	cup cilantro leaves
½	TBSP red pepper flakes
2	tsp ground cumin
1	tsp salt
¼	cup olive oil

Process all ingredients in a food processor until finely chopped. (if using a small food chopper, mix all ingredients and process in batches).

Marinate meat 3-5 hours.

If you are cooking a fresh ham, roast in the oven, on a rack, 4 - 4 ½ hours in a 325 degree oven.

Oriental Marinade

This is excellent for flank steak. Marinate flank steak overnight in a gallon bag, and grill 8 minutes on each side for rare.

1	cup soy sauce
½	cup brown sugar
2	TBSP minced, fresh ginger (or 2 tsp ground ginger)
2	TBSP minced garlic
2	TBSP chopped green onion

Marinades Using Store Bought Products

Zesty Italian Marinade

1	bottle zesty Italian dressing
¼	cup lemon juice
1	TBSP dried oregano
1	TBSP dried parsley flakes
2	tsp red pepper flakes

Mojo Marinade

1	cup mojo marinade
2	TBSP chopped cilantro leaves
2	tsp chopped garlic
1	tsp cumin powder
2	TBSP lime juice
2	TBSP minced onion

Caesar Marinade

This marinade is excellent for chicken breast. My good friend, Susi, used to make this chicken, and my kids loved it. The chicken breast is cut in half, marinated 1 hour, and cooked, in a sauté pan on high heat, browning nicely.

1	cup creamy Caesar salad dressing
¼	cup white wine
2	TBSP olive oil
2	TBSP garlic powder

Mix all ingredients and marinate meat in a shallow dish, covered in the refrigerator.

Marinara Sauce

I use this sauce as a base for Italian meatballs and sliced, cooked Italian sausage.

1	(32 ounce) can tomato sauce
1	(15 ounce) petite diced tomatoes
2	TBSP canned tomato paste*
1	TBSP sugar
2	TBSP chopped garlic
2	tsp dried basil
1	tsp oregano
1	tsp thyme
1	TBSP chopped, fresh rosemary

Combine all ingredients in a large pot and simmer for 30 minutes. Add desired ingredients** and serve with cooked pasta.***

* Use a 6 ounce can and freeze the rest in an ice cube tray, putting cubes in a freezer bag after frozen. Each cube should be approximately 1 TBSP. Use frozen cubes as you need them.

** Add any of these ingredients to create your own sauce. Feel free to add any ingredients that you like to this list to personalize your sauce.

Cooked, sliced Italian sausage

Cooked Italian meatballs

Cooked, sliced mushrooms

Cooked sliced onions

Cooked green peppers

Cooked zucchini

*** Spaghetti, penne, rigatoni, spiral, etc.

PORK OR CHICKEN WITH CREAM OF MUSHROOM SOUP

Both meats are so tender when this dish is served. My paternal grandmother is the one who first served this to me. I have made it many times at the sorority house, and my own kids love it.

4	boneless pork chops or 4 boneless, skinless, chicken breast
2	TBSP olive oil
1	can cream of mushroom soup
1	tsp garlic powder
1	TBSP parsley flakes
¼	cup beef broth or chicken broth*

Brown the meat, on each side, in a sauté pan in the oil. Put the meat in a baking dish. Add the mushroom soup to the pan and whisk. Add the broth, garlic powder and parsley. Whisk to mix well. Pour over the meat. Bake in the oven, 350 degrees for 1 hour.

If you have a crock pot, this recipe is wonderful cooked in a crock pot on low, for about 5 hours.

* You can substitute white wine for the broth.

Prosciutto and Pasta

This recipe tends to be very salty due to the prosciutto and olives, but it is delicious.

¼   pound thinly sliced prosciutto ham, chopped

1   small can sliced ripe olives, drained

¼   cup diced onion

¼   cup sodium free chicken broth

2   TBSP white wine

2   TBSP heavy cream

2   TBSP shredded Parmesan cheese

1   TBSP olive oil

1   TBSP butter

½   pound cooked angel hair pasta

Heat oil and butter in a sauté pan. Sauté the onion for about 5 minutes. Add procchuto and olives. Add heavy cream, white wine and chicken broth. Simmer 10 minutes. Add the Parmesan cheese and simmer 1 minute. Add the pasta to the pan and toss with tongs and serve in individual plates. Garnish with additional Parmesan cheese.

Note Can also be served as a first course, just use smaller quantity on the plate.

PUFF PASTRY PIZZA

1   puff pastry sheet, thawed

½   cup ricotta cheese

¼   cup shredded mozzarella cheese

2   TBSP grated parmesan cheese

¼   cup pizza sauce

¼   cup chopped pepperoni

1   egg mixed with 2 TBSP water (egg wash)

Mix the ricotta cheese, mozzarella and parmesan cheese.

Place the puff pastry on a lightly floured work surface. Roll out to a 12 x 16 inch rectangle. With the short side facing you, spread the cheese mixture over the pastry, leaving a 1 inch space all the way around except the side furthest from you, leaving 3 inch space on that side. Drizzle the pizza sauce over the cheese. Sprinkle with the pepperoni. Brush the 3 inch gap with some egg wash. Roll up jelly-roll style and place on a parchment lined sheet pan seam side down. Stretch the ends down and tuck under. Brush with egg wash and bake in a 400 degree oven for 25 minutes until golden brown. Take the roll out of the oven and let rest 10 minutes. Slice into 4 inch pieces and serve.

Add ¼ cup cooked, crumbled Italian sausage if you want.

SALMON IN PUFF PASTRY

A very impressive presentation. Looks complicated, but is easy and delicious. Serves 2.

2	(6 ounce) pieces salmon, skinned
1	sheet puff pastry, thawed
½	cup softened cream cheese
1	small jar pimentos, drained
2	tsp chopped Italian parsley
½	cup frozen, chopped spinach, squeezed dry
1	egg plus 1 tsp water

Beat the egg and water in a small mixing bowl, set the egg wash aside.

Mix the cream cheese, pimentos and parsley.

Roll out the pastry sheet a bit and cut into quarters. Working with one quarter, place one of the salmon pieces on top. Spread ¼ cup cheese mixture on top of the salmon. Layer ½ of the spinach on top of the cheese mixture. Brush the bottom layer of pastry (around the salmon) with the egg wash. Place another quarter of pastry on top of the salmon and bring down to meet the bottom layer of puff pastry. Cut the puff pastry with a pairing knife to within ½ inch of the salmon. Using a fork, seal the pastry by pressing into the two pastry sheets with the flat side of the fork. Repeat with the second salmon fillet. Brush both puff pastries with the egg wash and place on a baking pan lined with parchment paper. Bake at 350 degrees for 20 - 30 minutes until the pastry is golden brown and puffed.

Let rest 5 minutes and serve.

VARIATIONS

Omit the spinach and use arugula leaves instead.

Use Dill weed instead of parsley.

Use chopped mushrooms instead of pimento.

SHRIMP AND ANGEL HAIR PASTA

This is a wonderful "date" meal, served with a nice salad and French bread.

½	pound shrimp, peeled and de-veined
2	TBSP olive oil
1	TBSP butter
2	TBSP chopped garlic
½	cup diced tomato
¼	cup fresh basil, chiffonade
¼	cup white wine
¼	cup heavy whipping cream
2	TBSP grated Parmesan
½	pound cooked angel hair pasta, drained

Heat oil and butter in large sauté pan. Add the garlic and sauté 2 minutes, add the shrimp and sauté until the shrimp is pink. Add the tomatoes, cook 2 minutes. Add the white wine and cream, cook 2 minutes. Add the basil and cheese. Heat for 2 more minutes. Place the pasta on 2 plates and spoon ½ of the shrimp mixture over the pasta. Serve with additional Parmesan cheese.

SPAGHETTI CASSEROLE OR CAVATINI

This is a nice dish to take to covered dish suppers.

1 ½	pound ground beef or chicken
1	pound bulk sausage
1	cup chopped pepperoni
2	TBSP olive oil
1	cup chopped onion
2	TBSP chopped garlic
2	(14 ounce) cans petite diced tomatoes
1	(15 ounce) can tomato sauce
1	(6 ounce) can tomato paste
1	can sliced mushrooms, drained (optional)
1	TBSP oregano
1	TBSP basil
2	TBSP parsley flakes
1	cup shredded mozzarella cheese
1	cup shredded cheddar cheese
1	pound cooked, drained and rinsed in cold water spiral pasta

Brown the sausage and ground beef (or chicken) in a pan, crumbling it. Drain in a colander lined with paper towels, set over a paper plate. In a soup pot, heat the olive oil. Sauté the onion and garlic 5 minutes. Add the drained mushrooms, tomatoes, tomato sauce, tomato paste and herbs. Stir to incorporate all ingredients. Simmer 10 minutes. Add the ground meat and sausage. Add the pepperoni and pasta. Stir to combine. Spoon sauce into a deep baking pan that has been sprayed with non-stick spray. Bake, covered with foil 30 minutes. Carefully uncover and sprinkle the cheese on top. Bake an additional 15 minutes.

Remove the casserole form the oven and let rest about 10 minutes before serving.

SPECIALTY PIZZAS

Some suggestions for various pizza combinations. Use the already made crust or a store bought crust.

WHITE PIZZA

Brush crust with 1 TBSP olive oil

¼	cup basil pesto
½	cup feta cheese
½	cup mozzarella cheese
¼	cup sliced tomatoes or sun dried tomatoes, or both
2	TBSP pine nuts
½	cup diced cooked chicken breast (optional)
2	TBSP roasted red peppers (optional)
¼	cup chopped artichokes (optional)

MEDITERRANEAN PIZZA

¼	cup pizza sauce
¼	cup sliced Greek olives
2	TBSP roasted red pepper
¼	cup caramelized onion
¼	cup chopped artichoke
2	TBSP sun dried tomatoes
½	cup feta cheese
½	cup mozzarella cheese
½	cup cooked chicken breast or shrimp, chopped

Mexican Pizza

Mix

2   tsp ground cumin and 2 tsp chili powder and ¼ cup into 2 TBSP pizza sauce

½   cup cooked chicken breast, chopped or cooked shrimp

½   cup frozen corn, thawed

¼   cup green peppers

2   TBSP chopped jalapeno peppers (optional)

2   TBSP sliced black olives

¼   cup black beans, drained and rinsed

½   cup shredded cheddar-jack cheese

Bake and serve with sour cream.

Blue Cheese and Grape Pizza

¼   cup crumbled blue cheese

¼   cup sliced red grapes

½   cup shredded mozzarella

¼   cup caramelized onions (optional)

Sprinkle the mozzarella cheese over the shell. Scatter the grapes over the cheese. Sprinkle the blue cheese on top. Bake in a 425 degree oven for 10 minutes.

CARIBBEAN PIZZA

Add

2	TBSP lime juice 1 tsp ground cumin, ½ tsp ground ginger and
1	TBSP chopped cilantro to the pizza sauce
½	cup cooked chicken breast or shrimp
2	TBSP chopped green onion
¼	cup pineapple chunks
¼	cup diced red pepper
2	TBSP finely diced jalapeno peppers (optional)

Add any ingredients to the pizza crust and bake.

MARGHERITA PIZZA

An Italian classic. Named for Margherita of Savoy who became the queen of Italy. The colors of the pizza represent the flag of Italy.

2	TBSP olive oil
½	cup sliced fresh Buffalo mozzarella
1	Roma tomato, sliced thin
6	fresh basil leaves, chiffonade
2	TBSP shredded Parmesan cheese

Brush the crust with the olive oil. Layer the mozzarella cheese on the crust. Layer the tomato slices on top of the cheese. Bake in a 425 degree oven for 15 minutes. Sprinkle the pizza with the basil and Parmesan cheese.

THAI CHICKEN PIZZA

Mix

2   TBSP peanut butter with 2 tsp soy sauce, 2 tsp lime juice, 1 tsp minced garlic and 1 tsp ground ginger. Mix ½ cup chopped, cooked chicken with the peanut butter mixture.

1   TBSP vegetable oil

2   TBSP chopped green onion

¼   cup sliced red onion

¼   cup cashew pieces

2   TBSP chopped cilantro

1   TBSP fresh chopped basil

Brush the crust with the oil. Spread the chicken over the crust. Add the green onion, red onion and cashews to the top. Bake at 425 degrees for 10 minutes. Sprinkle with the cilantro and basil before serving.

Stir Fry

I love to make a stir fry. The prep is the difficult part. It involves chopping and dicing vegetables and meats. It is such a healthy meal that I don't mind the effort. Prep enough for several meals and your work is cut in half. Store prepared ingredients in storage bags in the refrigerator.

2	cups fresh mixed vegetables (snow peas, baby carrots and broccoli)
1	cup sliced mushrooms
1	bunch green onions, cut into into 1 inch pieces
3	celery stalks, cut into 1 inch pieces
1	TBSP Vegetable oil
1	TBSP butter
2	TBSP minced Ginger
1	TBSP minced garlic
2	TBSP soy sauce
2	cups diced chicken breast, shrimp or steak, uncooked and marinated in ¼ cup soy sauce and 1 tsp ground ginger

Cut the snow peas into 3 pieces. Cut the broccoli into small bite sized pieces and cut the carrots in half length-wise. Place in a mixing bowl. In a large sauté pan heat the oil and butter over med-high heat. Sauté the carrot, broccoli and snow peas, shaking and stirring the pan to evenly cook the vegetables for about 5 minutes. Add the celery, garlic and ginger. Sauté 2 minutes more. Add the mushrooms and green onion and sauté 5 minutes. Add the soy sauce. Remove pan from heat. In a separate sauté pan heat 1 TBSP oil on high heat. Sauté the meat in batches, stirring to brown all sides. Cook chicken until completely cooked. Beef does not need to be fully cooked, if you like it rare. Cook shrimp until opaque. Add the meat to the vegetables and heat, stirring until hot.

Serve with cooked Jasmine rice

Variation Add ½ cup finely sliced napa cabbage, ½ cup sliced bok choy, ½ diced zucchini, or ½ cup fresh bean sprouts.

Instead of meat, use diced, firm tofu.

Sweet and Sour Meatballs

I made this dish quite frequently in my early years. It takes a while to prepare, but it is so good.

1	egg
1	TBSP flour
½	tsp pepper
1	pound ground beef or chicken
½	cup vegetable oil
½	cup chopped onion
⅓	cup beef broth
1	(14 ounce) can pineapple chunks, drained (reserve ¼ cup juice for the sauce)

Whisk the egg in a mixing bowl, add the flour and pepper. Whisk the egg and flour until well combined. Shape the meat into walnut sized balls. Heat the oil in a fry pan on medium heat. Dip the meatballs into the batter and place them carefully in the fry pan. Brown on all sides. If you have some batter left, pour that into the pan as well. Drain the meatballs on a paper towel. Cool the oil in the pan slightly. Drain the oil from the pan by carefully pouring it into an empty can placed in the sink. (pre-drain the pineapple for the sauce and use the empty can, with a paper towel stuffed inside).

Reheat the pan on medium heat. Add the onion and cook 5 minutes. Add the pineapple chunks and ⅓ cup beef broth. Cook 10 minutes. Add the meatballs and heat 5 minutes. Pour the prepared sauce over the meatballs.

Sauce

¼	cup corn starch
2	tsp soy sauce
¼	cup cider vinegar
¼	cup reserved pineapple juice

½   cup sugar

½   cup beef broth.

Mix all the ingredients in a sauce pan, whisking until thickened. Be sure to whisk constantly, or frequently, to keep lumps from forming.

Serve with white rice.

Sides

I have included some favorite side dishes.

Baked Potato

I know this seems basic, but I had several sorority ladies ask me how to properly bake a potato.

To get a nice crisp skin on the potato, this is what I do.

2   baking potatoes

Scrub the potatoes to get all dirt off. Dry off. Poke holes through the skin with a fork, about 2 times. (this is to allow steam to escape and avoid the potato from exploding). Rub the potatoes with a little oil, if desired and sprinkle with kosher salt. Bake in a preheated 400 degree oven for about 45 minutes to an hour, placing the potatoes directly on the oven racks. Carefully remove the potatoes with pot holders. Split them open and put on desired condiments.

> sour cream
>
> steamed broccoli
>
> sauteed mushrooms
>
> cheddar cheese
>
> butter
>
> bacon bits (real)
>
> Chopped chives or green onion

To make twice baked potatoes use the following instructions.

Allow the potatoes to cool. Cut the potatoes in half length wise. Scoop out the inside of the potatoes, and place the potato pulp in a large bowl. Reserve the potato skins. Add 2 TBSP melted butter, ¼ cup sour cream, ¼ cup shredded cheddar cheese, 2 TBSP half & half, 1 tsp salt and ½ tsp pepper. Blend all ingredients with a hand mixer. Spoon* ½ of the mixture into each potato skin. Can be prepared to this point in advance. Store in the refrigerator until ready to bake. Place the potatoes on a parchment lined baking sheet. Sprinkle the potatoes with 1 tsp paprika. Bake in a 350 degree oven for 25-30 minutes.

* You can also place the potato mixture in a gallon size baggie, cut a 1 inch hole in one corner, and pipe the potato mixture into the skin.

GLAZED CARROTS

1	small bag baby carrots
¼	cup butter, melted
¼	cup brown sugar
1	TBSP yellow mustard
1	TBSP chopped parsley or 2 tsp dried parsley

Boil the carrots in water for about 15 minutes. Meanwhile, melt the butter, brown sugar and mustard together in a microwave. Whisk to combine well. Drain the carrots when they are tender, return to pot and add the glaze. Toss with a rubber spatula to coat. Sprinkle with parsley and toss. Serve immediately.

GORGONZOLA RIGATONI

My sister-in-law introduced me to this wonderful dish! It is perfect with grilled chicken.

¼	pound gorgonzola cheese
⅓	cup milk
3	TBSP butter
½	cup heavy whipping cream
½	pound cooked rigatoni pasta, drained

Melt the gorgonzola cheese, milk and butter in a sauce pan. Add the heavy cream and simmer about 10 minutes until reduced somewhat and thick. Add to hot pasta and serve.

Green Beans

Green beans make a nice green side dish for most main courses. I like to keep my beans whole instead of snapping them in half or thirds. I also use harcouverts, which is a small, thin green bean. You can find already trimmed and bagged green beans in the produce section, just be sure that they are fresh. Harcouverts can also be found in the produce section in a small bag.

¼   pound picked through green beans, trimmed, or bagged

        water to cover beans in a pot

1   tsp salt

1   TBSP butter

Bring water to a boil in a sauce pan, or pot, and add the beans. Simmer beans for about 10 minutes until they are tender but still crisp and green.

Drain beans in a colander. Return beans to the pot and add the butter. Toss the beans to coat with butter. (or melt the butter first in the microwave and drizzle over the beans). Serve hot.

Basil Green Beans

2   tsp dried basil

1   basic green bean recipe

Sprinkle the basil over the beans and toss to coat.

GREEK GREEN BEANS

1   basic green bean recipe, omit the butter and keep beans in the colander

1   TBSP olive oil

¼   cup diced onion

¼   cup diced tomatoes

2   TBSP finely chopped garlic

½   tsp oregano

2   tsp lemon juice

Heat the oil in a sauté pan. Sauté the onion for 2 minutes, add the garlic and cook 2 minutes. Add the beans and saute 5 minutes. Add the tomato, oregano and lemon juice. Cook to heat (about 2 minutes) and serve.

SOUTHWESTERN STYLE GREEN BEANS

1   basic green beans recipe, omit the butter and leave the beans in the colander

2   TBSP finely chopped onion

2   tsp finely chopped garlic

1   TBSP olive oil.

½   tsp ground cumin powder

½   tsp chili powder

Heat the oil in a sauté pan. Sauté the onion on med-high heat for 2 minutes. Add the garlic and green beans, cooking another 5 minutes. Add the cumin and chili powder. Toss to coat and serve hot.

CARIBBEAN GREEN BEANS

1	basic green bean recipe
2	tsp olive oil
2	TBSP finely chopped garlic
¼	cup diced onion
½	tsp ground cumin
2	TBSP lime juice
1	TBSP chopped, fresh cilantro

Heat the oil in a sauté pan. Add the onion, garlic and beans. Sauté about 5 minutes. Add the cumin, cilantro and lime juice. Heat about 2 minutes and serve.

ORIENTAL GREEN BEANS

1	basic recipe green beans, omit butter and leave beans in the colander
1	TBSP vegetable oil
1	TBSP finely chopped ginger (or 1 tsp ground ginger)
1	TBSP finely chopped garlic
2	TBSP chopped green onion (optional)
1	TBSP soy sauce

Heat the oil in a sauté pan on med-high heat. Sauté the beans for 5 minutes. Add the garlic and ginger. Sauté 2 more minutes. Add the green onion and soy sauce. Continue to cook, tossing the beans for 1 minute more. Serve hot.

Green Beans Almondine (green beans with almonds)

1   basic green bean recipe
¼   cup toasted almond slivers

Add the almonds to the pot and toss to coat. Serve hot.

Spicy Green Beans

1   basic green bean recipe
2   tsp olive oil
1-2   tsp red pepper flakes
1   tsp dried oregano

Add all ingredients in a pot and heat, tossing for 2 minutes. Serve hot. Goes with Italian meals.

Curried Green Beans

1   basic green bean recipe
1   tsp curry powder
¼   tsp ground ginger
        sprinkle of garlic powder

Add all ingredients to a pot and heat, tossing to coat, 2 minutes. Serve hot.

SOUTHERN STYLE GREEN BEANS

½ pound green beans (whole or snapped in half or into thirds)
   water to just cover the beans

2 -3 TBSP bacon grease

¼ cup chopped ham (optional)

1 TBSP salt

¼ tsp ground pepper

Bring all ingredients to a boil in a pot. Lower heat and simmer, covered, 30 minutes.

POTATOES

There are so many ways to prepare potatoes. I am only including some of my favorites.

BAKED POTATOES

2   baking potatoes, washed and poked with a fork a few times

Preheat the oven to 400 degrees. Place the potatoes in the oven, directly on the rack. Bake for 45 minutes. You will have a nice crisp skin.

If you do not like a crisp skin, you can bake the potatoes in the microwave for 4 minutes, turn and bake another 4 minutes or so.

PAN FRIED POTATOES

1   baking potato, peeled and sliced into thin rounds
½   TBSP olive oil
½   TBSP butter

Heat the oil and butter in a large saute pan on med-high heat. Place the potato rounds in the pan in one layer. Cook the potatoes turning frequently to brown on both sides. Lower the heat to low and cook another 5 minutes.

Roasted Potatoes

2	baking potatoes*, peeled and cut into wedges
2	TBSP olive oil
1	TBSP minced garlic
1	TBSP chopped, fresh rosemary

Mix all ingredients in a large bowl, tossing to coat the potatoes. Sprinkle with 1 tsp kosher salt and 1 tsp ground black pepper. Spread the potatoes in a single layer on a baking pan sprayed with non-stick spray. Roast in a 400 degree oven for 15-20 minutes, stirring half way through the cooking time.

*You can also use whole small red potatoes, quartered large red potatoes, fingerling potatoes or wedged russet potatoes.

MASHED POTATOES

2	baking potatoes, peeled and cubed
½	cup half & half
1	tsp salt
2	TBSP butter

Cook the potatoes in boiling water in a medium sauce pot until tender. Drain the potatoes and put back in the pot. Add the butter, half & half and salt. Mix with a hand mixer until well blended. Add more half & half if needed.

Variation Add any or all of the following

2	TBSP sour cream
½	cup shredded sharp cheddar cheese
2	TBSP chopped green onion
1	TBSP sauteed minced garlic

Rice

There are thousands of ways to prepare rice. Rice is very versatile. Rice can be used as a side dish or as a main dish when meat is added. I have several rice dishes that I prepare for the sorority, which I have listed here.

Basic Rice

I use long grain rice or Uncle Bens converted rice. Use 1 part rice to two parts of liquid.

1	cup rice
2	cups water
1	tsp salt
1	TBSP butter

Bring the water to a boil in a sauce pan with a lid, add the rice, butter and salt. Lower the heat, cover and cook on low for about 20-25 minutes. Serves about 2 people.

Sometimes I'll bake rice in the oven. Some of the recipes I have included here call for baking.

Fried Rice

I don't actually fry this rice, but it is wonderful served as a side dish or with cooked shrimp, chicken or pork added after you have made the rice.

2	cups rice
4	cups water
1	tsp salt
3	TBSP vegetable oil
1	cup mixed vegetables thawed and sauteed in a bit of vegetable oil
2	tsp ground ginger
¼	cup soy sauce

Put the rice in a sauce pan. Add the oil and stir the rice so that it is coated with the oil. Add the water and salt, bring it to a boil. Lower heat, cover and cook 20 - 25 minutes.

Sauté the vegetable mix (small peas, carrots, beans, corn and lima beans) in the oil. Add the ground ginger to the vegetables. When the rice is done, add the vegetables and soy sauce to the pot. Stir with a rubber spoonula. Add cooked shrimp, chicken or pork if desired.

A good use for leftover meat. Before adding meat, marinate it in some soy sauce and ground ginger for additional taste.

MEXICAN RICE

This rice is good as a side item or used as a filling for fajitas or tacos.

3	cups water
1 ½	cup white rice
2	tsp salt
1	TBSP olive oil
1	cup frozen corn, thawed
½	cup diced onion
¼	cup diced green pepper
1	TBSP chopped garlic
1	TBSP chili powder
1	tsp cumin powder
1	tsp oregano
¼	cup salsa

Combine the rice and olive oil in a large sauce pan 3 quart), mix to coat rice with oil. Add the water and bring to a boil. Cover the pan, lower heat to low and simmer 25 minutes. Meanwhile sauté the corn, onion, peppers and garlic in a sauté pan for 10 minutes.

Remove the rice from the heat. Add the corn mixture and salsa and mix well using a rubber spoonula. Sprinkle the chili powder, cumin powder and oregano over the rice. Mix well and serve.

Store any leftovers in the refrigerator for 3 days, or freeze in individual freezer bags and defrost as needed.

BROWN RICE

2	cups beef broth
1	cup rice
2	TBSP butter
½	cup chopped onion
¼	cup chopped fresh mushrooms (optional)

Combine all ingredients in a covered baking dish that has been sprayed with non-stick spray. Bake in the oven at 350 degrees for 45 minutes.

Serves 2.

LEMON RICE

This rice is amazing. It is so simple, but makes a great side dish and requires no sauce or gravy to make it good.

2	cups chicken broth
1	cup white rice
1	whole garlic clove
1	TBSP butter
2	TBSP lemon zest

Spray a sauce pan with non-stick spray. Add the chicken broth and bring to a boil. Add the garlic clove and rice. Lower heat to low, cover and cook for 20 - 25 minutes. Take off heat and add the butter. Let sit for 2 minutes, add the lemon zest, stir and serve.

Yellow Rice with Peas

I serve this rice as a side dish for fish. It is also good with cooked chicken or shrimp added to it.

2   cups water or chicken broth

1   TBSP olive oil

1   cup yellow rice

1   cup frozen peas, thawed

Combine the rice and oil in a sauce pan. Add the liquid and bring to a boil. Lower heat to low, cover and cook 25 minutes. Add the peas to the rice and stir gently with a robber spoonula.

Roasted Sweet Potatoes

The sweetness of the potatoes work well with the cayenne pepper.

2	sweet potatoes, peeled and cubed or cut into strips
2	TBSP olive oil
1	TBSP chopped fresh rosemary
1/	tsp cayenne pepper
1	tsp salt

Place the potatoes in a bowl and toss with the rosemary and oil. Single layer the potatoes in a baking pan sprayed with non-stick spray. Sprinkle with the cayenne pepper and salt.

Roast the potatoes in a 400 degree oven for 10-15 minutes.

SPINACH

A lot of spinach makes a little amount.

1   bag baby spinach

1   TBSP olive oil

Heat oil in a large sauté pan. Add the spinach and cook, turning the leaves around in the pan using tongs. Sauté until the spinach is wilted.

Variation Add 1 TBSP minced garlic to the oil before adding the spinach. Sauté the garlic 1 minute and add spinach.

SWEET POTATO CASSEROLE

3   sweet potatoes, peeled and cubed*

⅔   cup brown sugar

2   eggs, slightly beaten

1   tsp vanilla extract

½   cup sweetened condensed milk

½   cup melted butter

Cook the sweet potato in a pot of boiling water about 15 minutes. Drain and cool slightly.

With a hand mixer beat the potato brown sugar, butter, condensed milk, egg and vanilla until well mixed and smooth. Spoon the potato mixture into a rectangular baking dish that has been sprayed with non-stick spray. Sprinkle with the following topping and bake in a 325 degree oven for 30 minutes.

Can be prepared a day in advance, covered and stored in the refrigerator. Bring to room temperature before baking, or bake an additional 10 minutes if you bake right out of the refrigerator.

Topping

½   cup brown sugar

⅓   cup all purpose flour

¼   cup butter, softened

1   cup finely chopped pecans (chopped in the food chopper)

½   tsp cinnamon

With a hand mixer, beat all ingredients on low until well blended and crumbly.

* You can use canned, mashed or cubed sweet potato.

Breakfast

I have included just a few dishes for breakfast which are mostly make ahead recipes.

BAKED FRENCH TOAST

A wonderful make-ahead brunch casserole.

1	24 inch baguette (about 4-inches in diameter)
6	eggs
3	cups whole milk or half & half
1	tsp vanilla extract
¾	cup brown sugar

Cut the baguette into 20 one inch slices. Place the slices in a 13x9 inch buttered baking pan (or spray the pan with nonstick spray). In a blender mix the eggs, milk, vanilla and brown sugar. Pour evenly over the bread slices. Cover and keep in the refrigerator over night.

To bake preheat the oven to 350 degrees. Melt ½ stick butter with ¼ cup brown sugar in a sauce pan. Whisk to blend well and drizzle over the bread. Bake 25 minutes, uncovered. Cool slightly and cut into squares. Serve with syrup and powdered sugar.

Variation Prior to baking sprinkle about 1-2 cups blueberries and 1 cup pecans over the bread.

CHEESE GRITS

An absolute favorite of the sorority girls!

2	cups quick grits
2	cups water
2	cups half & half or whole milk
¼	cup butter
2	tsp salt
1	tsp garlic powder
2	cups shredded sharp cheddar cheese

Bring the water, half & half , salt, garlic powder and butter to a boil. (watch the pot carefully because when milk boils, it will boil over) Add the grits and lower heat to low. Whisk often to keep the grits from clumping. Cook about 5 minutes whisking often. Add cheese, stir well, cover and cook another 10 minutes, whisking frequently. Add more milk if the grits get too thick. Remove from heat and keep covered. Grits will stay warm for quite a while.

Sometimes I'll add 4 ounces of softened cream cheese for extra richness.

SHRIMP & GRITS

Everyone, here in the south, has their own way of making shrimp and grits. I made mine many times for the girls. Shrimp and grits can be served as a breakfast, brunch, lunch or dinner dish. It good paired with Patti's salad.

I have made this dish 3 ways **1)** adding all ingredients together (as I do in this recipe), **2)** serving the grits and shrimp separately or **3)** folding in stiffly beaten egg whites to all ingredients and baking in the oven for 30 minutes (this produces a souffle' effect which will allow the dish to stay light and fluffy for transportation).

1	pound shelled and deveined shrimp (medium size)
½	cup chopped onion
½	cup chopped green pepper
1	TBSP chopped garlic
¼	cup chopped tomato
1	TBSP chopped parsley
2	TBSP butter
1	tsp old bay seasoning
1	TBSP flour
¼	cup white wine
1	recipe prepared cheese grits

Sauté the onion and pepper in the butter for 5 minutes. Add the garlic and sauté 2 more minutes. Sprinkle in the flour and stir to incorporate. Add the tomato, parsley, old bay and wine. Stir in the shrimp and turn off heat. Add a pinch of pepper and cayenne pepper if desired. Add all ingredients to the grits. Heat the grits on low until the shrimp are just barely pink. Serve in bowls or on a plate.

MUFFINS

Start with a basic muffin mix and make various muffins.

Pour the batter into muffin pans that have been lined with muffin cups. Bake as directed on the muffin package.

CRANBERRY NUT MUFFINS

½   cup dried cranberries (craisins)
½   cup chopped nuts walnuts or pecans

BANANA NUT MUFFINS

(use about ¼ cup less liquid when mixing the batter)

½   cup mashed bananas
½   cup chopped nuts walnuts or pecans
1   tsp cinnamon
½   tsp vanilla extract

APPLE CINNAMON MUFFINS

(use about ¼ cup less liquid when mixing the batter)

½   cup apple sauce
¼   cup sour cream
2   tsp cinnamon mixed with 1 TBSP sugar
½   cup chopped walnuts (optional)

CINNAMON RAISIN MUFFINS

½   cup raisins

1   TBSP cinnamon mixed with 3 TBSP sugar

¼   cup chopped walnuts or pecans (optional)

ORANGE MARMALADE MUFFINS

(use about ¼ cup less liquid when mixing the batter)

½   cup orange marmalade

Add ½ cup cranberries for extra zest

BLUEBERRY MUFFINS

⅔   cup fresh or frozen (thawed) blueberries

CHOCOLATE CHIP MUFFINS

⅔   cup chocolate chips or white chocolate chips (or both)

Drop about 5 chips on top of the muffin after you have poured in the batter.

You can add ½ cup chopped pecans to the batter before pouring for a chocolate nut muffin.

PINEAPPLE MACADAMIA MUFFINS

(use about ¼ cup less liquid when mixing the batter)

½   cup crushed pineapple
½   cup chopped macadamia nuts
¼   cup flaked coconut (optional)

BANANA SPLIT MUFFINS

(use about ½ cup less liquid when mixing the batter)

½   cup mashed bananas
¼   cup crushed pineapple
¼   cup chopped maraschino cherries
½   cup chopped walnuts

CHERRY ALMOND MUFFINS

½   cup chopped maraschino cherries
½   cup sliced almonds (toasted)

PECAN AND BROWN SUGAR MUFFINS

¼   cup brown sugar
½   cup chopped pecans
1   tsp vanilla extract

Now that you have the idea, try creating your own combinations!

SAUSAGE AND EGG CASSEROLE

This casserole was a tradition in my house on Christmas morning. It is a wonderful make ahead dish.

6	slices white bread, cubed
1	pound bulk sausage (I like Jimmy Dean)
2	cups shredded sharp cheddar cheese
6	eggs
2	cups milk
1	tsp dry mustard

Put the sausage in a sauté or frying pan. Cook and crumble until brown. Drain sausage on paper towels.

Put the bread cubes in a 9x13 baking pan, sprayed with non-stick spray. Sprinkle the sausage evenly over the bread. Sprinkle the cheese over the sausage. Whisk the eggs, milk and mustard together until well blended. (can be mixed in blender). Pour the egg mixture evenly over the casserole. Bake at 350 degrees for 25-30 minutes.

Can be made ahead of time. Cover and refrigerate overnight. Bake, uncovered as directed.

Sweets

I have a few sweets that I love to make. I don't do many sweets in my diet, but every once in a while it is nice to have a sweet treat or dessert for a party.

CHERRY-O CHEESE PIE

I am not a huge fan of cheese cake. Cherry-O pie is not as dry as cheese cake and has a wonderful creamy texture. My mom used to make it when I was a child.

1	(9 inch) graham cracker crust
2	TBSP melted butter
1	(14 ounce) can sweetened condensed milk
1	(8 ounce) package cream cheese, softened
¼	cup lemon juice, fresh or bottled
1	tsp vanilla extract
1	(14 0unce) can cherry pie filling

Brush the pie shell with the butter and bake for 10 minutes in a 325 degree oven. Cool completely before filling. In a mixing bowl, beat the cream cheese with a hand mixer on medium until fluffy. Mix the condensed milk in gradually. Stir in the vanilla and lemon juice. Pour into cooled pie shell. Cover with the pie shell top and chill at least 3 hours to set the filling. To serve, spread on the cherry pie filling and cut into slices. Alternately you can cut the pie into slices, place on a plate and top with some pie filling.

Sometimes you can find the miniature graham cracker crusts; these make cute individual pies. Follow the same directions, just even out the pie filling into each shell.

Chocolate Purses

1   sheet puff pastry, thawed

2   cups chocolate morsels (semi sweet)

1   cup white chocolate chips

1   cup chopped pecans

Place the puff pastry sheet on a lightly floured work surface. Roll the pastry into a 14 inch square. Cut the square into 4 equal squares. Place ½ cup chocolate morsels, ¼ cup white chocolate chips and ¼ cup pecans in the center of each square. Bring the corners up to meet in the middle, twist the edges to form a pouch with a fluted top (similar to a draw-string pouch) . Place the purses on a parchment lined sheet pan. Bake in a 375 degree oven for 15 - 20 minutes. Remove from oven and let rest about 5 minutes. Serve as dessert on small plates.

Variation

Use 1 cup raspberry flavored chocolate morsels and just 1 cup chocolate morsels.

Use 1 cup Heath Bar chips instead of the white chocolate, or use ¼ cup Heath Bar chips and ¼ cup white chocolate.

DUMP CAKE

This is the easiest and most delicious dessert ever.

1	box yellow cake mix
2	(14 ounce) cans diced peaches, 1 can drained
½	cup chopped pecans
1	stick butter

Pour the peaches in a 9 x 13 casserole pan sprayed with non-stick spray. Sprinkle the dry cake mix on top of the peaches, evenly covering them. Spread cake mix so that it is smoothed down. Cut the butter into ¼ inch pats. Evenly distribute the pats over the cake mix. Sprinkle the pecans over the top. Bake in a 350 degree oven for 30 minutes.

Serve with cool whip or vanilla ice cream.

VARIATION

Add 2 cups mixed berry frozen fruit, thawed, to the peach layer.

Put 2 cans crushed pineapple, ½ cup brown sugar and ½ cup drained maraschino cherries in the bottom of the pan.

Put 2 cans cherry pie filling in the pan and top the cake mix with slivered or sliced almonds.

Key Lime Pie

I have had key lime pie since I was a kid. I lived in St. Petersburg Florida where the key limes were fresh off the trees. I have found that the store bought key lime juice is a good substitute.

1	can sweetened condensed milk
½	cup key lime juice
3	egg yolks
1	graham cracker crust
1	TBSP melted butter
3	egg whites
2	TBSP granulated sugar

Brush the crust with the butter and bake in the oven at 325 degrees for about 5 minutes. Cool while preparing the filling.

Using a mixer, mix the egg yolks, lime juice and condensed milk together. Pour into the crust and bake 10 - 15 minutes at 325 degrees.

Cool the pie on a cooling rack.

Mix the egg whites and sugar together on high speed until stiff peaks form. Spread the egg white mixture on the pie filling. Bake 5 minutes more until a bit golden on top. Chill in the refrigerator at least 2 hours.

Miscellaneous

In this section I have included some ideas for uses of puff pastry and phyllo cups. I also have some menu ideas using the recipes in the book.

PUFF PASTRY

Puff pastry is one of my most favorite things to use for so many different foods. It can be used in savory and sweet dishes for appetizers, salads, main dishes, breakfast foods and desserts. I have included numerous recipes which use puff pastry. The ideas are endless. Puff pastry is very easy to use and is very forgiving. It can make any dish look expensive, complicated and delicious, when in actuality it is quite easy. Puff pastry is found in the dessert section of the freezer area in a grocery. It comes in two forms; sheets and shells. Sheets are ideal for wrapping ingredients in and for placing on top of dishes such as pot pies and some casseroles. Shells are good as containers for saucy foods, creamy foods and custards.

There are so many uses for puff pastry, aside from the recipes I include in this book. Look up puff pastry recipes on the internet to find additional recipes.

Puff Pastry Shells

There are so many uses for these shells. Bake the shells according to directions. Scoop out the inside and add these ingredients, per one shell.

Chicken Pot Pie

½   cup cream of chicken soup
¼   cup frozen mixed vegetables (peas, corn, lima beans, green beans & carrots) thawed
½   cup chopped, cooked chicken (use left over chicken)

Heat all ingredients in a small sauce pan for about 15 minutes. Spoon over a warm pastry shell.

Beef Pot Pie

Spoon left over beef stew over a warm shell.

Chili Pie

Spoon left over chili over a warm shell. Add sour cream, shredded cheddar and green onions.

Seafood Pie

½   cup store bought alfredo sauce

¼   cup cooked shrimp

¼   cup cooked scallops or canned crab meat

1   TBSP finely chopped green onion

¼   tsp black pepper

1   TBSP white wine

Heat all ingredients in a sauce pan for about 10 minutes. Spoon over a warm shell and sprinkle with shredded parmesan cheese.

Salad Pie

Fill with strawberry spinach salad mixture and serve as a salad course. (or any salad mixture).

Sweet Ideas

Spoon the following into a cool shell

Chocolate or vanilla pudding. Top with whipped cream and strawberries (or other berries).

Lemon pudding topped with whipped cream and blueberries.

Apple pie filling topped with whipped cream or vanilla ice cream.

Strawberry pie filling topped with whipped cream.

Chocolate flavored whipped cream, drizzled with chocolate sauce, topped with strawberries or raspberries.

Whipped cream cheese mixed with sour cream, topped with cherry pie filling.

All of these are just suggestions. I am sure you can come up with many of your own ideas.

Puff Pastry Sheets

Roll out a defrosted oastry sheet and add these ingredients on top. Roll up the pastry, seal the edges, brush with egg wash and bake at 350 for 30 minutes. Cut roll into desired slices.

- 1 cup pizza sauce, ½ cup shredded mozarella cheese, ½ cup chopped pepperoni. (additionaly you can add chopped green peppers, chopped onion, crumbled Italian sausage)

- Spread sheet with 1 cup cream cheese, spread on top of this ½ cup Major Grey's Chutney, sprinkle with 1 cup cooked, crumbled bulk sausage.

- Spread sheet with ½ cup cream cheese mixed with ¼ cup sour cream and ¼ cup shredded monterey jack cheese and 2 TBSP salsa. Sprinkle ½ cup chopped, cooked chicken and any of the following sliced black olives,chopped green onion, chopped tomatoes or chopped cilantro. (you can sprinkle with taco seasoning before rolling up)

Phyllo Cups

This wonderful little item can be found in the freezer section of your grocery store. Generally it is in the dessert area. It is a product made of phyllo dough and is pressed and baked into small cups. I have used phyllo cups in many different ways, but the one I love most is for appetizers. You can keep a package in your freezer and use them as needed. You can fill these cups with just about anything you can imagine. Whatever you have on hand can work. If you are going to fill them with something cold, bake them a while prior to filling, or you can fill them and then bake. When making the cheese recipes, put a small chunk in the shell before adding the other ingredients.

Let your imagination run wild, and use what you like. I have made a few suggestions in the following recepies, but anything goes!

BRIE

(all of these should be baked for about 5 minutes before serving)

Brown sugar and chopped pecans

Crystallized ginger and a piece of fresh pear

Jalapeno and sliced date

Orange marmalade and sliced almond

Chutney (Major Grays, a mango chutney which is expensive but can be stored for a long period of time and has other uses)

Dried cranberries and chopped walnuts

Sliced red grape and chopped pecan and maybe a sprinkle of chopped fresh rosemary

Duck breast and dried cherries

As you can tell, I like Brie with sweet and nutty or spicy hot. I think it is a perfect vehicle for these flavors. Many of the above combinations also work well with Cream of Havarti cheese

SOUR CREAM

(bake the cup before filling)

A dab of salsa and a sliced ripe olive, a jalapeno slice, chopped green onion or s cilantro leaf

Smoked salmon and chopped green onion or capers

Smoked salmon and dill weed

Cooked shrimp and salsa

FETA CHEESE

(bake before or after filling, your choice)

Slivered sun dried tomato and basil (fresh or dried) add toasted pine nuts

Chopped olive (of your choice, I like calamata) and basil or sun dried tomato

Store bought pesto and a small piece of cooked chicken breast or shrimp

Grape tomato (halved) and Greek olive (pitted)

BLUE CHEESE OR GORGONZOLA

(bake before or after filling)

Sliced red grape

Chopped walnuts or pecans

Small piece of leftover steak or chicken

Chopped figs and walnut

CREAM CHEESE

(bake before or after filling)

Nova Salmon and dill weed (fresh is preferable) (bake before filling)

Roasted red pepper (from a jar) and chopped spinach (fresh or frozen, thawed) (bake after filling)

Orange marmalade and cooked chicken breast (bake before filling)

Cooked shrimp and salsa, cocktail sauce or Major Grays Chutney (bake before filling)

SWISS CHEESE AND CHEDDAR CHEESE

Granny Smith apple and walnut (bake cheese in cup then add fruit and nuts)

Pear and walnut (bake cheese in cups then add fruit)

Pecan and bacon (bake after filling)

Salad Fillings

Any of my chicken salads can be put into a phyllo cup for a nice appetizer. Do not bake the shells at all, just thaw, fill and serve. Garnish with a parsley sprig,

Sweet Combinations

(Bake before filling)

> Cream Cheese mixed with a bit of sour cream and cherry pie filling
>
> Chocolate whipped cream (canned in the refrigerator section) and sliced strawberry or raspberries
>
> Strawberry cream cheese and blueberries
>
> Vanilla pudding and banana
>
> Vanilla pudding and maraschino cherry
>
> Vanilla pudding, flaked coconut and pineapple tidbits
>
> Lemon pudding and blueberries (you can also use lemon curd, found in the baking section)
>
> Pistachio pudding and maraschino cherries

At this point, I could go on and on. You get the idea, just use your imagination and make your own combinations according to what you like!

Menu Ideas

Grilled cheese & cream of tomato soup

Chicken salad criossiants & spinach salad

Minestrone & Stacie's Mediterranean salad

Shrimp & grits with Patti's salad

White chicken chili & corn bread salad

Krab salad sandwich with sweet & sour slaw

Individual beef wellington with green beans almondine & pan fried potatoes

Salmon in puff pastry with asparagus & yellow rice

French herb chicken with brown rice & leseuer peas

GLOSSARY

I have included some definitions of terms which I use in this book, or I think are important for you to know.

al dente: Pasta cooked until it is firm to the bite. For most cooks, it is the preferred consistency for pasta. Personally I like my pasta a bit more done.

all-purpose flour: Flour suited for most cooking and baking purposes. I like to use unbleached.

baguette: A long, narrow loaf of French bread. I like to use a baguette, sliced thin, for appetizers.

balsamic vinegar: A pungent yet sweet and mellow vinegar. This is truly a multi-purpose vinegar and one of my favorites.

blanch: Placing food (usually vegetables) into boiling water for a few minutes to crisp cook them, then into ice water to stop the cooking process.

cheese cloth: Cotton gauze that does not fall apart when it gets wet. Cheese cloth is used to strain liquids. I use it to squeeze thawed, chopped spinach.

chiffonade: Thin strips of vegetable leaves. To chiffonade basil, place leaves one on top of the other. Roll the leaves into a loose roll. Slice through the leaves with a sharp knife, creating thin strips.

chop: To cut food into pieces, ranging in size; large, medium, small and fine.

cider vinegar: A fruity vinegar made from fermented apple cider.

colander: A metal or plastic bowl-shaped container with small holes for draining foods.

core: To remove the woody or seeded center of fruit such as apples, pears and pineapples.

corn starch: A powdery white substance used as a thickening agent for sauces. Corn starch won't add any flavor to a dish, only consistency.

cutlet: A thin, tender, boneless cut of meat. Usually turkey, chicken, veal or pork. To make it extra tender, pound the meat out by placing it between two sheets of wax paper and pounding it with a meat mallet.

deglaze: An easy way to make a reduction sauce. After sauteing meat, remove it from the pan and add a small amount of liquid (broth, cream, wine, apple juice, etc.). Whisk the liquid until well blended and reduced. This creates an intense flavor for a sauce.

dice: To cut food into very small cubes.

dredge: To lightly coat food with flour, cornmeal or bread crumbs.

fold: To incorporate a light fluffy mixture, such as beaten egg whites or whipped cream, into a heavier mixture. I use a large spoon shaped rubber spatula to fold ingredients.

marinate: To soak food in a seasoned liquid mixture. The purpose of marinating food is for the food to absorb the flavor of the marinade. Marinating meats will help to tenderize it.

garnish: To add something extra to a plate for additional flavor and appearance. A garnish should always be edible and enhance the flavor of the dish.

parchment paper: Grease-resistant paper used for lining baking sheets. Parchment paper keeps food from sticking.

paring knife: Small, sharp knife with about a 3 inch blade. A paring knife is a good all-purpose kitchen knife.

puff pastry: Layered pastry dough. Puff pastry can be found in the dessert freezer section of your grocery store. Puff pastry comes in sheets or shells.

puree: To finely blend food to a smooth consistency. You can use a food processor or blender. I prefer to use a blender.

reconstitute: To rehydrate a dried food by soaking it in a liquid.

reduce: To cook a liquid over high heat to decrease its volume. This produces the flavor of the liquid to intensify.

render: To cook a food (bacon, ham, panchetta, beef, etc.) on low heat until it releases its fat.

roux: (Pronounced ROO) A mixture of flour and fat that is cooked over low heat, used to thicken mixtures such as soups and sauces. I usually use butter for my roux.

sauté: To cook food in fat (olive oil, oil, bacon grease or butter) until nicely browned.

score: To cut shallow lines in a diamond shape, on meat or fish.

sear: To cook meat quickly over intense heat to form a crust.

strain: To remove unwanted particles from a liquid by pouring through cheese cloth or a metal strainer.

stir fry: To quickly fry small pieces of food in a large pan over very high heat while constantly stirring the food.

whisk: A utensil that is made up of a series of looped wires. It helps to keep sauces, cream soups, grits and other such foods from forming lumps. A whisk is excellent for making dressings and sauces. To use a whisk, practice doing this; jiggle your wrist back and forth. Place the whisk in your hand and make the same motion.

Made in the USA
Monee, IL
28 April 2022

95555808R10121